Pro
Cre

Santiago

Grimes Pos
3362

This Miracle

"For this cause
the people also met him
for that they heard
that he had done
this miracle."
(John 12:18 KJV)

This Miracle

Stories edited and compiled
by Joan Hileman

This Miracle

Printed in the United States of America through Lightning Source.

Amlin Publishing Paperback edition / May 2008

Amlin Publishing Paperbacks are published by Amlin Publishing Inc. through Lightning Source, a subsidiary of Ingram Industries Inc.

Contents

I Am Here, Mary's Story	8
Good Things, Bryon and Ruthie's Story-	11
The Door, Lisa's Story-	14
All Things, David's Story-	19
Judgment Day, Ken and Jeanette's Story-	36
Distance, Ruthie's Story-	43
The Hiding Place, Herb and Flo's Story-	45
The Sobering Truth, Bob's Story-	48
Little Warrior, Eryn's Story-	59
Jolted, Dave's Story-	88
Katahdin, Jamie's Story-	89
Our Daily Bread, Laura's Story-	92
The Cross, Larry's Story-	94
Erika's Angels, Erika's Story-	97
Pierced, Nancy's Story-	104
Make It Blue, Stephanie's Story-	114
Take My Hand, Sandy's Story-	115
That Still Small Voice, Jean's Story-	120
The Nurse's Aide, Marie's Story-	121
A Simple Prayer, Autumn's Story-	126
Take My Life, Jeremiah's Story-	128
From Dealer to Healer, Chuck's Story-	136
The Appointment, Kim's Story-	149
Salt and Light, Elizabeth's Story-	153
Heaven, Lily's Story-	159
The Gift, Joan's Story-	161
My Shield, Daniel's Story-	164
Tracy's Song, Joanie's Story-	166

Foreword: *Me?* Write a Book?

By J. Hileman

I'm not trained as a writer, and I never finish long projects, so when I felt the Lord was telling me to write a book of miracles, I was doubtful. —But He was persistent, and I was convinced. Here's how it happened.

In 2001, at a Calvary Chapel service, Pastor Ken Graves mentioned miracles. He was teaching from the book of Luke when he started chasing a rabbit and found himself up in a tree with a coworker. The coworker said, "I ain't never heard of no miracles happening around here." But Ken said, "I've heard of hundreds of miracles."

But that's where he left it, and instead of telling us about miracles, he suddenly jumped out of the tree and started walking back towards the subject, leaving me on the edge of my seat. Miracles in Bangor, Maine? I wanted to know about them!

So when the book *My God Story,* from Calvary Chapel Fort Lauderdale came out, I bought it and read it. *Twenty-six people. Twenty-six stories. One God.* It's a book of miracles, and it's very good.

Then all of a sudden, I started having this thought: *I should write a book like that.* Time and time again the thought came to me. So I prayed, "*God?* Are *You* putting this thought into my head? Or is this just me trying to find a way to get attention?"

I should write a book like that. (There it is again.)

"Lord, I know I'm a decent writer, and I think writing is fun and all, but if you want me to write a *whole book*, I need to know for sure."

I should write a book like that.

The thought wouldn't leave me alone. BUT, I didn't want to say anything, because if I told people about it—then I might actually have to *do* something.

Finally the thought tortured me enough that I just had to tell someone! And when I told my friend, Nancy, her enthusiasm surprised me. She said, "My heart just filled with JOY when you said that! What an *awesome* idea! What an *amazing* way to tell people about the Lord!"

So I interviewed Nancy, who just happened to have a story to share, but it took *months* to write up the rough draft—and I did a terrible job. Clearly I was imagining things. God hadn't spoken to me.

But the thought kept returning: *I should write a book like that.*

And then—a different kind of thought. *Who am I kidding? It's obvious I don't have time for this. What will I have to sacrifice to get it done? my kids? my house? I'll waste years of my life and no one will publish it anyway. Forget it. It's a TOTAL waste of time.*

So I pretty much gave up the idea, until one day when I was reading a *Focus on the Family* magazine. A scripture jumped right off the page, smacked me in the head, and jumped directly into my heart. "... be ye steadfast, unmovable, always abounding in the work of the Lord, forasmuch as ye know that your labor is *not in vain* in the Lord." (1 Corinthians 15:58, emphasis added.)

So I finished a story, but it took a *long* time, and another thought started haunting me. *Look how long it took to write one little story. I can't write a whole book! This is stupid. This is a GIANT, huge, big honkin' thing. And I never finish long projects. Remember the quilt? and that cross stitch thing that's been in the drawer for fifteen years? I'LL FAIL. I'll never get it done.*

Then, right on cue, Pastor Ken taught us a new song. "The GIANT's calling out my name and he laughs at me, reminding me of all the times I've tried before and failed. The giant keeps on telling me time and time again (girl) you'll never win. You'll *never* win. But the voice of truth tells me a different story." *I should write a book like that.* "The voice of truth says do not be afraid." *Your labor is not in vain in the Lord.* "The voice of truth says this is for My glory. Out of all the voices calling out to me, I will *choose* to listen and believe the voice of TRUTH."

Alright already! I'll stop listening to the voices of doubt, and I'll listen to Your voice only, Lord. I WILL write that book—

—juuust as soon as I get caught up with my housework.

So every night, at around nine, I would gather up the few brain cells that were still awake, and together we'd sit in front of the computer, not doing much of anything.

Until one Sunday morning at church, the Lord spoke loud and clear to my spirit. In an almost audible voice, I heard, *"You need to sacrifice your house."* A moment later Matthew 6:33 came to mind. "But seek first his kingdom and his righteousness, and all these things will be given to you as well." I took this to mean that I needed to put the book first, and that somehow my other work would get done.

So now, I get my kids off to school, spend some time in the Word— then I walk past the dust, and the kids' nightclothes on the floor, and the breakfast dishes, and the laundry, and the toys... and all the other STUFF that never goes away no matter how much you work at it. And I sit down at my computer, and all of my rested little brain cells and I work together to edit miracle stories! Then later, when my brain is completely fried, I work on housework. (Did you know it only takes two brain cells to fold laundry, and one and a half to vacuum?)

So even though I might have to live in a less than perfect house (BIG giant understatement) and it might take me twelve months to get the Christmas decorations down, I have found amazing satisfaction and peace, in *finally* submitting to the will of God!

It took two years to get through to me, 'cause I'm not the smartest knife in the drawer, but I finally realized that God can use *anyone* to do *anything,* if only we are willing to take his hand, and go where he leads. And if you are holding a finished copy of *This Miracle* in your hands, it's all God's work— because I'm not trained as a writer, and I never finish long projects.

"being confident of this,
that he who began a good work in you
will carry it on to completion..."
(Philippians 1:6 NIV)

The following stories fall into
five basic categories;

angel stories,
salvation,
healing,
God's provision,
and God's protection.

Some contain elements of more than one of these categories. The large majority occurred in or near central Maine. In only a couple have the names been changed for confidentiality purposes. While a few may not be as *miraculous* as the rest, they are still touching stories of how God's people have been moved to show His love in amazing ways. To the best of this writer's knowledge, based on the moral character of the people who shared their stories, as well as documents, etc., the stories are true.

And one more thing, finding these miracles was not difficult. Although miracles can happen to anyone at anytime, as far as this writer can tell, they are relatively common among those who have chosen to surrender their lives to the Lord Jesus Christ.

A big hug to Nancy,
for her unparalleled enthusiasm.
A warm thanks to all the precious people
who shared their miracles.
And my heart, my soul, my all, to my God,
who hasn't given up on me yet.

I Am Here

Mary's Story

The sky was overcast and the smell of rain was in the air when we got the call.
Union Street. Car accident. A bad one.
We bolted for the ambulance. It was 9:30 PM.
Noise. Noise at the scene. *So loud.* Sirens *blared.*
Traffic backed up. Rescue workers shouted to be heard above the NOISE.
Even still, I could hear her.
A two year old. Lying in the street.
Screaming. Screaming. ***Screaming!***
A woman knelt by her. Holding her head.
Gently. Firmly.
Don't move, Dear One. Don't be afraid. I am here.
I ran to her side. "Keep her still! Can you keep holding her! I need more equipment!"
The woman nodded. So calm. So very calm.
I got the equipment. We secured her. And it was time to move.
Still the woman helped. We carried her, ever so slowly, *so slowly,* the few yards to the ambulance—one, inch, at a time.
"Don't let her move her head!"
Be calm, Little One. Precious Child. I am here.
The girl had quieted a bit by the time we got her into the ambulance.
I set to work quickly, stabilizing her, securing her.
Quickly.
It was pouring rain now.
The woman stood outside the ambulance.

In the pouring rain.
Watching. Listening.
As I secured the child, the woman spoke up.
"Would it be alright if I left now?"
She stood in the rain.
Yes. I told her yes.
She could go. I was all set. Thank you.
Back to my work. Several seconds passed, and I looked up. I needed to get her name, she deserved more. She deserved a reward!
I looked out the back of the ambulance.
I looked out the windows. The lights were bright, they lit up the whole area.
I should have been able to see her walking away.
But she was gone.

Two doctors in Bangor, and one in Boston, all said the same thing.
"Why is this little girl alive? She should have died."
Her neck was broken.
She should have died.
But she didn't.
Someone was holding her.
Holding her still.
Still. Be still, Little One.
I am here.

Mary believes this woman was a guardian angel— and it's not the first time she has had this thought.

Jesus said,
***"Take heed that
ye despise not one of these little ones;
for I say unto you, That in heaven their angels
do always behold the face of my Father..."***
(Matthew 18:10 KJV)

Angels, ministering spirits, continually riveted on the face of the Father, waiting on the edge of their seats, for the next command to head for the ladder.

***"...and behold a ladder
set up on earth, and the top
of it reached to heaven: and behold
the angels of God ascending
and descending on it."***
(Genesis 28:12 KJV)

Good Things

Bryon and Ruthie's Story

Relocating to a new state with seven children during a recession wasn't the easiest thing in the world to do, but time and time again, God was faithful to provide.

One Christmas, I found myself unemployed, and Ruthie and I found ourselves at the Good Will store, trying to buy gifts for seven kids with twenty dollars. As you can imagine, it was hard finding anything, that was worth anything, in the piles of *junk* that had already been picked over. But we managed to find seven junky little toys so our kids would at least have *something* to open on Christmas morning.

Feeling depressed and desperate we took the long way home, and started looking for money along the side of the road. I had remembered a story my grandfather told me about a time when he was desperate for money. His car had broken down, and he'd found a hundred dollars on the road. So as we rolled slowly along, we scanned the roadside and saw something that looked like money blowing in the wind. But when we got out, we found it was only a piece of paper, and when we got back in, we were more depressed than ever.

We didn't think it was right to pray for gifts, because we know that Christmas is about Jesus. And besides, there were more important things we needed to be praying about; we hadn't paid the mortgage, we barely had enough money to buy food, and everyone needed clothes. But our hearts were broken. We desperately wanted our kids to be blessed on Christmas. So sitting there in the car, we cried and apologized, but then we asked the Lord to *please* bless our kids.

"And whatever we ask,
we receive from Him, because
we keep His commandments and do
those things that are pleasing in His sight.
And this is His commandment, that
we should believe on the name
of His Son Jesus Christ..."

(1 John 3:22-23 MKJV)

On Christmas Eve, the crappy little toys were sitting underneath the pathetic looking Charlie Brown tree we had found in the field. Ruthie and I were feeling about as horrible as we could possibly feel. But then the phone rang. It was a couple we had met once or twice, relatives of some church friends. We barely knew them, but they wanted to know if they could come over.

They arrived in a fifteen passenger van and came to the door and asked if the kids could help them carry in a couple of things. A *couple* of things! It turned out, the van's rear seats had been removed, and the whole vehicle was packed to the roof with packages! The kids brought in load after load until the little tree was *completely* buried and gifts were spilling out into the room. —And then they started hauling in groceries!

We didn't have enough money to buy a Christmas turkey, but they brought everything, boxes and boxes of food, enough for a huge Christmas dinner, and enough to last for awhile after that.

We will never forget what our six year old daughter, Callie, said as she stood in front of the open refrigerator. She said, "Look, Mom! We're rich with milk!" To this day, we still say this. We know if we can afford to buy milk, we're rich!

The next morning, when the gifts were opened, we didn't find cheap plastic toys from the grocery store. We found high quality, brand new toys, like thirty dollar Tonka trucks, and practical gifts like winter coats and boots. Someone had taken the time to find out the kids' ages and sizes, likes and needs, and everyone got exactly what they needed!

There were thousands of dollars worth of gifts and food, and to this day, we still don't know where it all came from. But as we stood there watching load upon load of good things being brought into our house, we felt like the Lord was saying, "*This* is my heart toward you. I *want* to bless you."

It *is* the Lord's heart to bless his children, and we now know, that our best, is nothing but junk, compared to what the Lord can do.

"If you then, being
evil, know how to give good
gifts to your children, how much more
shall your Father in heaven
give good things to those
who ask him."
(Matthew 7:11 MKJV)

The Door

Lisa's Story

On the outside, I looked the same, but on the inside,
I had changed so much, I didn't even know who I was
anymore. As I stood staring at myself in the mirror,
I remembered the day. That day.
That was when everything had begun to change!

We kept seeing this add on TV. This guy, an athlete, kept telling us how much his life had changed, and that if we ordered this book, it would change our lives too. So my husband ordered it. But then it just sat there on the shelf, and we never gave it another thought.

Until I found myself out of work, again, and I just *happened* to come across this book. I had plenty of time on my hands, with nothing better to do, so I started reading it. I don't remember the name of the book, but it had quotes from the Bible, and stories of how God had changed people's lives. And the one thing it kept coming back to, time and time again, was how there was this "door" people had gone through, and that this "door" was Jesus.

Jesus said, "I am the door:
by me if any man enter in, he shall be saved,
and shall go in and out, and find pasture."
(John 10:9 KJV)

As I read, I began to think about my life. It was a mess. My marriage was failing; my anger had caused me to lose yet another job; there were days when I was so depressed, all I wanted to do was drive off the road into a tree; and my drinking had gotten out of control. In fact, every night, I headed over to my next door neighbor's house to get drunk. I had been doing this for almost a year. As I read, I thought about how my life was a complete disaster— and I wondered about this "door."

At the end of the last chapter, there was a prayer, so I said it. I got down on my knees, and I prayed a prayer asking for Jesus to come into my heart and save me.

But I didn't feel any different.

So I got up and went on with my day, but the thing about the *door* wouldn't leave my mind, and it was still with me a short time later as I walked down to the end of my driveway. When I opened my mailbox, it was empty, except for one small postcard advertisement. In big letters, it said, "The Doors Have Been Opened." Two big golden gate doors were pictured on the front, and at the bottom it said, "Front Row Video."

I stared at this postcard all the way back up to the house, but then the phone rang. It was a friend of mine, and she told me about a job opening at a local restaurant. By the time I hung up the phone, the door, was forgotten.

I drove down to the restaurant and put in an application. The next day I was interviewed and got the job.

Slowly things began to change for the better. I still headed to my friend's every night, but I couldn't drink as much anymore; it made me feel sick. So my drinking slowly decreased and I didn't miss it. Then when my friend moved away, I stopped altogether.

My marriage was ending, and I was planning on quitting my job, but one of my coworkers encouraged me to stay. The very next day I was asked if I wanted to work in the bakery. It was here that I met Shaun. We became instant friends, and he started telling me about how God had changed his life.

As time went on my attitude became completely different. I was rarely angry anymore and I almost never got depressed. I stopped blaming everyone else for my problems, and I stopped being so focused on what *I* wanted all the time. More and more I started to really *see* people and appreciate them for who they were.

We began attending a little church down the street from my house, and it was here that my daughter asked Jesus into her heart. Soon after this, my sister and I, and our two daughters, were baptized.

Gradually Shaun and I became closer and started dating, and during this time, I kept thinking to myself how *lucky* I had become. Everything seemed to be going so well for me. But I chalked it all up to coincidence, until something happened that made me stop and think.

Just before Shaun and I were to be married, we were looking for a house. We needed something halfway between Thorndike, where Shaun was going to be working, and my daughter's house in Eddington. So we prayed about it. We asked God to help us find a nice place halfway between Thorndike and Eddington.

Every day, Shaun took the interstate to work, but on this particular day he decided to take it slow and drive up Route 9 instead. As he passed through Hampden, he saw a *For Rent* sign in the window of a house and called the number immediately. The man who answered the phone was amazed. He had just put the sign up that very minute!

Later that day we went and looked at the house, and it was *perfect.* A nice house in Hampden, and all the man wanted for rent was four hundred dollars. He didn't want any deposit and he said we didn't need to pay the rent right away if we didn't have it! It seemed too good to be true, but it *was* true, so we gladly told the man we'd take it.

Later that week, I measured the miles from Thorndike to Hampden to Eddington. The driveway of the house in Hampden, was *exactly* (to the tenth of a mile) halfway between Shaun's work and my daughter's house!

So I began to wonder if the things that were happening were more than just luck.

Then one day I found myself looking at my reflection in the mirror, and I couldn't believe how much I had changed. On the outside I looked the same, but on the inside, I had changed so much, I didn't even know who I was anymore, and suddenly I remembered the day. That day. It was the day I had gotten down on my knees and prayed for Jesus to come into my heart. *That* was when everything had begun to change! I had opened the door, *The Door*, and miracles had begun to happen.

"Therefore if any man be in Christ, he is a new creature: old things are passed away; behold, all things are become new."
(2 Corinthians 5:17 KJV)

So when you pray to God asking for something, and it happens, don't think it was just luck. No matter what it is, thank God for it, because He actually did do it. Come to the realization that He really does exist and that He really does care. Don't look for big giant miracles to take place. Don't wait for lightning to strike. Just thank Him for the small things. And when you finally acknowledge Him and say "Thank you, God," that's when He smiles and says, "No problem. I'll do it again."

The day I prayed that prayer, something real happened, even though I didn't feel it. Jesus says if you open the door, he will come in, and he means it. The day I prayed that prayer, Jesus stepped through the open door of my heart, and quietly began to work on me.

***Jesus said, "Behold,
I stand at the door and knock:
if any man hear my voice, and open
the door, I will come in..."***
(Revelation 3:20 KJV)

It's that simple.

All Things

David's Story

"I may have to go with your God theory—
because this cannot be explained medically."

David: Dear Lord, I would like to see a miracle here on earth. I know that you can perform miracles, but I just want to see one with my own eyes.

The phone call:

"Hello."

"Mrs. Chrisos. —Is David there?"

"Gosh, no, David's at school."

"No. No. He never showed up. —Some kids who just came up Broadway said there was a car just like David's. They're pretty sure it was David's car. And he was in a pretty bad car accident... Mrs. Chrisos?"

A moment later:

"Yeah."

"Don it's Terri! Where are you?"

"I'm right in town, heading out Broadway. Why what's wrong?"

"I just heard David was in a bad accident out past Kev-Lan. You should be there."

"What? What happened?"

"I don't know, I just heard it was bad."

"Alright. Okay. I'm almost there now."

When I arrived at the scene of the accident, the ambulance was already gone. I was thankful for the few minutes warning I'd gotten from Terri, because if I had seen my son's car unprepared, I would have lost it. It was teetering sideways on a four foot bank of ice on the opposite side of the road. The passenger side was flattened with the rear tire sticking out sideways. The bumper was hanging by one bolt and folded into a V, and where the rear window had been, a jumbled mess of interior jutted out. I pulled open the driver's side door and peered in. All but a small space around the driver's seat had been completely mangled.

David?

The five minute drive to St. Joseph Hospital felt like an hour. This can't be happening. This can't be happening. I can't believe this! Please let him still be alive. Oh God please don't let him die!...

When David's father arrived at the hospital, pastors from his church were already there with several others praying for David. The seventeen year old lay in critical condition, with blood, and bandages, and tubes coming out everywhere. But at least he was alive, and there was still time to pray.

As soon as news reached Bangor Christian School, high school classes were canceled, and people started praying.

After being moved to Eastern Maine Medical Center, David was given a CT scan. The results revealed a massive brain injury. David was given drugs to keep him in a coma in an effort to minimize further swelling in his brain. The next three days would be critical.

Every moment, at least one family member stayed by David's side. If it wasn't Mom or Dad, it was brother Jonathan, or Billy. Twenty-four hours passed and the neurologist became concerned. By this time, the swelling should have subsided and David should have been responding more. A second CT scan was ordered. David's brain was still swelling.

For three days, David remained in a drug induced coma. For three days, David breathed with the help of a respirator. And for three days, people continued to pray.

Finally the doctors decided it was safe to take David off the drugs, and the family waited anxiously for him to wake up. But he didn't.

Another day went by, and on Sunday afternoon, a nurse came in to talk with the family. "The waiting area is packed with people wanting to see David. We took the chairs out to make more room but they just keep coming. Do you want to come out and see them before we start sending them away? We just finished counting; there are 144 people out there."

Only two of the 144 were relatives. The rest were friends and people whose lives had been touched by David in one way or another. Throughout the day people continued to pack the waiting area, and since it was tournament time, entire basketball teams showed up to offer words of encouragement. One man, who had traveled all the way from Calais, summed up the general feeling. He told the family, "I'm not really surprised that David would draw this many people. It isn't because he's a great athlete, which he is, it's because he's a great kid."

A Great Athlete:

To say this high school junior was a great athlete was something of an understatement. As a captain for the Bangor Christian Schools' baseball team, David had been awarded the title Most Valuable Player two years in a row. As a captain for the golf team, he had been MVP three times, and had taken second in the state his junior year. As a captain for the basketball team, he had been chosen MVP twice, was a member of the Penobscot Valley All Star Team, and had been selected as one of Maine's Best Basketball Tournament Players.

From the time he started Kindergarten, David had been telling people that he and his friends were going to win the states in basketball for their small Christian school, and it had looked like that goal would be realized. As a starting guard his junior year, David lead the team in minutes played and had scored an average of sixteen points per game. The Patriots had just finished a 17-2 regular season and were in the number one seeding heading into the Eastern Maine Basketball Tournaments.

A Great Kid:

Not only did David excel in sports, but he was on the National Honor Roll, was the Junior Class Treasurer, the National Honor Society Vice President, and a student tutor. He was a volunteer for the Children's Miracle Network, The Salvation Army, United Way, the local soup kitchen, missions projects, and Vacation Bible School. And on top of everything else, he still found time to coach Pee Wee basketball and soccer.

For David, serving others was something that came naturally. David's mom reports, "From the time he was a little boy, David was always willing to help in any way he could. Whether he was doing household chores, visiting an elderly neighbor, or giving money to a homeless person, his sensitivity towards others was always apparent.

"David told us about a boy in high school. He said he always ate lunch by himself on the front steps because some kids had ostracized him for his weight. At least once a week, David made it a point to sit outside with this boy.

Some weeks he sat with him several days, and after awhile, other kids started joining them. One day towards the end of the year, David told me there were ten kids out there. —We knew David had a lot of friends, but judging by the number of people visiting the hospital, we saw that he had touched more lives than we ever imagined."

In the early hours of Monday morning, four days after the accident, David regained consciousness. Later that day, an MRI was taken. The results were devastating. David had sustained a "near fatal" brain injury. His frontal lobe, his rear lobe, and multiple areas in between were injured. The family was prepared to expect the worst. He would need to relearn many things, his personality might be completely changed, and he might never be able to live independently.

And people continued to pray.

"He's awake! He's awake!"

David's father ran back into the hospital room where he saw his son's eyes wide open— for the first time in four and a half days. David had an awful headache, but when his basketball coach entered the room, he immediately asked about their quarterfinal game. When he learned it was only a few hours away, he said, "I'll be up and running soon. I don't think I can start, but I'll give you a few minutes off the bench." This brought tears to his father's eyes, because here was the David he had always known. And he knew at that moment, they were going to have to chain this boy down, so he would have time to heal.

The nurse began to ask David questions about his age, where he went to school, where he lived, the positions he played in sports, and so on. David was able to answer *every* question. The nurse was *blown* away. She couldn't understand how someone with such extensive brain injury was answering questions as though nothing had happened. But when she asked him about the accident, he remembered nothing, except one thing he would later tell his parents.

"After my car was hit, God stretched out his hand, and I grabbed it."

When the Patriot's basketball team entered the Bangor Auditorium later that morning, David's number 34 was painted on faces, written on sneakers, and scrawled across banners throughout the stadium. Perhaps the biggest cheer of the game was heard during the introductions—when David's name was announced. David's teammates knew beyond a shadow of a doubt that he would want them to go on without him, because David did *not* like to lose. At all. The news of his waking inspired the Patriots to run faster, jump higher, and play with the most devastating press Bangor Christian fans had seen all season. The result was unrelenting pressure that caused fifteen unanswered points in the first quarter, forced twenty-one turnovers in the first half, and brought the team to a 79-54 victory. They were doing it for David, and they were NOT going to let him down.

David was happy when he heard about the game, but he was still fading in and out of consciousness, and he still didn't understand what had happened to him.

"Mom. Why am I here?"

"You had an accident."

"I did?"

"Yes."

"What happened?"

"You hit black ice."

"Oh. —Did I kill anyone?"

"No."

"Was Greg in the car?"

"No. He called and told you he didn't need a ride."

"Oh. —So I was the only one who got hurt?"

"Yes."

"—Mom?"

"Yes?"

"Am I in the hospital?"

"Yes."

"What happened?"

"You were in an accident."

"Was anyone killed?"

This went on for several days, but gradually David began to put the pieces together. "So I was in an accident. I hit black ice. Greg wasn't in the car. No one was killed..."

When David was told he would need to go through extensive physical, occupational, and speech therapy, a Bible verse entered into his mind, and he assured his parents that he was going to be just fine. In the days, weeks, and months to come, whenever he was faced with a new challenge, he gave his best effort, and rested in the promise, "I can do all things through Christ who strengthens me." (Philippians 4:13)

The first time David got up to take a shower, the nurse told the family they would need to explain everything to him step by step. She said to show him the soap and explain what it was for, etc., but when David got into the shower, he knew exactly what to do. He didn't need any help at all.

"I can do all things through Christ who strengthens me."

"...pray one for another, that you may be healed..."

(James 5:16 MKJV)

Eight days after the accident, a conference was called. The rehab doctor looked at the MRI and appeared baffled. He explained, "With such extensive injury to the brain, your son should not be doing what he is doing at such an early stage of recovery. I cannot explain this."

David's father piped up and said, "I can explain it. So many people have been praying for our son— and the Lord is answering our prayers."

The doctor didn't know what to think. He had been a rehabilitation doctor for over thirty years, and he had never seen anything like it. Finally, he said, "I may have to go with your God theory— because this cannot be explained medically."

When more scans were taken, only a few injured areas remained!

The family was told it would take a year for David to complete physical therapy. David finished in three and a half *weeks.* He made more progress in that time than most people with his kind of brain injury make in two years.

The family was told it would take two years for David to complete speech therapy. David finished in six months. At the end of the six months, the therapist said, with tears in her eyes, "When he can do better than I can, it's time to say goodbye." David had blessed her so much, she hated to see their time together come to an end.

In the spring, David went back to school for half a day. With the help of a tutor, he worked into the summer and was able to complete his junior year— with high honors.

The following was written by David's brother Jonathan and first appeared in the Bangor Christian School

Patriot's newsletter a few months after David's accident:

> It's amazing how a single event, a brief moment in time, an unexpected incident can change a person's life forever. It's amazing how God allows events to happen, how He helps us to understand that everything happens for a reason, and how He gives us amazing strength and peace to get through it.
>
> It was February 14, my first class was at 9:30, and I had plans like every other Valentine's Day to wallow in self-pity for not having "A Big Day of Love Fest" planned. At 7:58, while I was getting ready to go to class, a car, headed to 1476 Broadway, hit a patch of black ice, and spun out of control into oncoming traffic. The high impact collision left a BCS teenager unconscious and barely breathing.
>
> This would not be my typical Valentine's Day. To my chagrin, my wallowing was about to get a lot worse. Boycotting the patron saint's Valentine's Day and bemoaning an A- I received on a recent exam were about to move down the list in my directory of "The World's Greatest Problems."
>
> After we received the call – the call everyone hopes they never get – my mom and I bolted for the door and were off to Broadway. I was praying for a fender

bender, hoping for the best, not expecting the worst. When my dad called on the cell phone and told me, “It's bad. Go to St. Joe's,” I knew I needed to get prepared for the worst.

When we arrived at St. Joseph's, our pastors and some friends were already there, waiting for us to arrive. I don't know how exactly to describe the mood. Maybe “calm panic” would work. Except for my mom, her mood is easy to describe: panic heart-brokenness. Definitely nothing calm about it. The St. Joseph's people told us to go to the family room. There they would talk to us. At this point everyone who had gathered at the hospital began crying and my mom passed out. I suppose you mothers would understand.

In the family room, basically we found out they were doing some tests, and we really wouldn't know anything for a while. Oh, and it was a while! All we

could do was wait and pray and pray and pray. Did I mention we were praying a lot?

Finally, I asked a nun if I could go in and see my brother. That was a big mistake. I thought I wanted to see him, but in the condition that he was in, I should have stayed in the family room. I walked into his room in the emergency ward. He was just lying there. Tubes coming out from everywhere you can put a tube, head bleeding and bandaged, his clothes were in shreds on the floor. I

grabbed his arm, and although he was unconscious, we prayed together. It is a scene that will be etched in my memory forever.

After a couple of hours, he was transferred to EMMC where he would stay for three weeks. The first week he spent in the ICU, five days of it in a coma. For three weeks we continued to get news from the medical community that was not as positive as we would have liked. But what they did not realize, when they were quoting us statistics, is that we have an all-powerful Father in heaven on our side ... a Father who would be cheering for David every step along the road to recovery ... a Father who has been with David his whole life and was in the car the morning of February 14. I remember David telling my dad in the hospital, "When my car got hit, God reached out his hand, and I grabbed it."

David has never been bitter, never asked "why," and he has had an amazing testimony for the Lord. In fact, he thanks the Lord every day for saving his life and that the accident happened to him and not to one of his friends or family members. It hasn't been easy for him either. He works so incredibly hard every day to be even better than he was before his accident. I am proud to call him my brother. He inspires me every day and challenges me to look at the world differently.

While he was in the hospital, I had a lot of time to think. I thought too much actually. But I often wondered, unlike David, why this had to happen to him. I would think, “He's a good kid, and he didn't deserve this.” I know many other people thought this as well. A very wise woman in my church gave me a remarkable answer. “When God was looking for someone for this to happen to, He knew David could handle it and would be a good witness and example for Him. It's an honor.”

WOW! I wasn't expecting that. I asked her if she thought David would be okay. Another good answer, “No matter the outcome, remember that God is always good. Sometimes He is gracious. I am praying that He will be gracious.” WOW again. God *is* good, and He has also been gracious.

Now that David is home and doing so well, I have been doing some more thinking. Oh no, here we go. Why did our family, friends, church community, even strangers drive, fly, and travel from all over the state and country to be with us? Why did they sit for hours in the hospital waiting room when they knew there was nothing they could do? Why did we receive countless cards, meals, balloons, and flowers? Why are people still praying for David?

People are good and people are loving. No – people are incredible. From our entire family, thank you, everyone!

Although I didn't realize it at the time, Valentine's Day 2002 taught me that love is more than a dozen over-priced roses, a cupid-shot arrow through the heart, an expensive meal, or a Britney Spear's valentine that says, "I hope your Valentine's Day is a big hit!" Love is people pulling together and praying, visiting, and crying for hours at a time with a family who is going through a rough time. Love is God sending an angel to be with someone when they need it most. Love is cards, meals, and flowers from a sincere heart. I learned more about love. I learned to appreciate life and enjoy every moment of it. I learned that sometimes it takes a tragedy to bring people to their knees in prayer. Although I didn't realize it at the time, "A Big Day of Love Fest" *was* planned – people from all over showed their love to the Chrisos family.

"I'm sure you hear it all the time, but how's Dave doing?" It's a question I never mind answering because it gives

me a chance to talk about three really cool things: the love of God, my "miracle boy" little brother with the awesome attitude, and the goodness of people. David always wanted to see a miracle on earth. Not only did he see one, he is one. David shouldn't have been able to go back to school this year; he shouldn't have been able to be on the high honor roll; he shouldn't be able to ace tasks in therapy, and he shouldn't be able to play basketball this summer. But he has done all these things, and he will be playing this summer! Go number 34 ... Maine loves you, and we are proud of you! Thank you, God, for being good ... and gracious. It's amazing how a single event, a brief moment in time, and an unexpected incident can change a person's life forever.
—Jonathan Chrisos

The following year, instead of trudging his way through physical therapy, David was back to playing golf, basketball, and baseball. He was All State in all three sports. In his first basketball game since the accident, David scored 13 points, including the game-winning basket. For the rest of the season, he averaged fourteen points per game, and before the season was over, he reached the 1,000 point mark for his high school basketball career.

During his final year in high school, David was a student tutor, a teacher's assistant, a coach for Pee-Wee basketball, Treasurer for the Fellowship of Christian Athletes, Vice President for the National Honor Society, and was voted Who's Who among America's high school students. He also volunteered with the Booster Club, the local soup kitchen, Vacation Bible School, Praise Puppets ministry, The Children's Miracle Network, The New York City Missions Project, and the Baseball Dugout Project.

"I can do all things through Christ who strengthens me."

Out of approximately 14,000 student athletes who were nominated for the 2002 Wendy's High School Heisman Award, two seniors from Bangor Christian Schools were chosen as state finalists. David was one of them. They were asked to write an essay about one of their heroes. David wrote about his father. The other BCS finalist wrote about David. From the New England states as well as New York, a winner was chosen to represent the northeast region. David was that winner.

By the end of his senior year, only sixteen months after his accident, David received over $200,000 in scholarship offers and was accepted at every college he applied to including the prestigious Wheaton College, which has been called, "the Harvard of Christian colleges." He received a full academic scholarship to Eastern Nazarene College in Massachusetts where he went on to play three years of college basketball as one of the team's top players. He has kept up a grade point average of 3.5 or better, and continues to touch the lives of others through volunteer opportunities.

Recently, David proposed marriage to his girlfriend of two years, and she said, "Yes."

Because of his accident, David's lifelong dream of winning the high school basketball state championship was never realized, but he was never bitter. In fact, he is actually thankful for the accident and he will gladly tell anyone who will listen, "My recovery was a miracle; the very miracle I asked the Lord to allow me to witness. He is the reason I am here today and I hope to touch people's lives by telling them what God has done for me. Some people think my healing was luck, but I tell them no. People prayed for me, and God did a miracle. If my story is bringing people closer to the Lord, then I would gladly go through it all over again."

Just this last semester, as a senior in college, David earned a grade point average of 4.0. And David says,

"I can do all things through Christ who strengthens me."
(Philippians 4:13 MKJV)

David's car.

David helping mom with the vacuuming.

Judgment Day

Ken and Jeanette's Story

Ken: The elevator doors opened, and there was Tom.
I wanted to kill him. Just get in, close the doors,
and *KILL him.*

Jeanette: Once again it was time to put Micah on the plane to go visit his father. Once again I worried about his care and safety. And once again I cried. He was my baby, only nine years old, and he had to travel from Maine to California by himself, to spend the entire summer with the man who had abused me for years.

Tom had never abused our son, but because of his lifestyle and involvement with drugs, I worried constantly. At best, Tom would be a bad influence. At worst, well, I would try not think about the worst.

So Ken and I hugged our boy one last time, prayed again that the Lord would watch over him— then watched as he boarded the plane.

Tom vowed to make Jeanette's life miserable if she ever left him, and he threatened revenge if she took Micah away. But after nine years of abuse, despite the threats, she decided to leave. She filed for divorce— and the court awarded her full custody of Micah.

Tom stayed true to his word; he stalked her, he threatened her over phone, and he took her to court five times trying to win custody of his son. Even when she married a pastor and moved to Maine, he still found ways to harass her.

The day after we put Micah on the plane we received a phone call from our lawyer in California. Micah had been *severely* beaten. Tom had taken several photographs of Micah showing cuts and bruises all over his body. Our lawyer had seen them; he said they were real. And Tom was accusing *Ken* of child abuse!

I was *panicked.* Micah was fine when we put him on the plane. Something *horrible* had happened! But, *what?* Was he assaulted on the plane? Was there some kind of accident? Did *Tom* do this?

Ken: I wanted to kill him. He was behind this, there was no doubt. He was always making threats, detailed threats about burning people with acid or breaking their bones... One time he had even hired a thug to beat up a teacher, because he gave him a bad grade.

So I figured he would do something dirty like this. And I wanted to kill him.

Jeanette: Was Micah okay? Would Ken be convicted of child abuse? Would I lose custody of my son? What would happen with the church? And what about Jessica, our new baby? Would DHS try to take *her* away?

We called our Maine lawyer immediately. All he could say was, "I don't know what's going on here, but pray hard, and get to California."

So we prayed. I fell on my face before the Lord and begged him to get us out of this. The next day we called everyone we knew and asked them to pray. We had people over to the house for prayer, and I even called the 700 Club. They were having a telethon, and when I called, they prayed for us right there on the show. So people all over the nation heard about us, and were praying.

And Ken called Tom.

Ken: I still wanted to hurt him. I was torn up constantly, *frustrated,* and enraged that anyone would accuse me of abusing a child, especially this particular child. I loved Micah. But I had to *choose* to put my anger aside, and I had to *choose* to leave things with the Lord; *He* would take care of things. So I called Tom, and I told him what the scriptures have to say about what he had done.

"He who digs a pit shall fall into it,
and he who rolls a stone shall
have it turn back on him."
(Proverbs 26:27 LITV)

"The wicked have laid a snare for me;..."
(Psalm 119:110 KJV)

"...but the wicked shall fall by his
own wickedness."
(Proverbs 11:5 KJV)

Jeanette: Getting on that plane to face charges of child abuse was probably the hardest thing I have ever done. Here I was. I had everything, and in a matter of minutes it could all be gone. The evidence against us was strong, and our lawyers said there was nothing we could do.

So we prayed for a miracle.

When we arrived at my mother's house in California, she told us our lawyer had called and wanted us to go to his office right away. There was new evidence against Tom! We were allowed to witness the evidence but were told to say *nothing* about it; what had been a civil case, was now a criminal case, and if Tom found out about it, he was sure to skip town, and we would probably never see him, or Micah, again.

The next day at the courthouse when the elevator doors opened, there was Tom and his lawyer. I thought Ken was going to kill him.

Ken: I wanted to kill him. Just get in, close the doors, and *KILL him.* The lawyer took one look at me and started frantically pushing buttons to get the doors closed. After this, they didn't want me in the courtroom at all. But finally someone asked if I would ever hurt a woman, and when I said, "No!" they decided to let me go in with a female secretary on each arm.

Jeanette: First the judge announced that new evidence had been brought forward, and then Tom's lawyer stood up and said he was resigning from the case. Tom stared at him with a look that said, "*What!?*"

A woman came through the doors, walked up the aisle, and handed the judge a tape. Tom was *panicked!* He stood up and said, "Your Honor, I resign, I don't want to press charges, I don't..."

But the judge told him to, "*Sit* down!"

He put the tape in the player, looked at Tom— and pressed play. A woman's voice could be heard.

"That's how you made those bruises was with grease pencils?"

The judge bent the microphone down to the speaker.

"Yes, we used grease pencils." (That was Tom's voice.)

"I thought you said you used putty?"

"Yes, putty and grease pencils. To get the creases in the broken skin, we used putty..."

Ken: It was like a vision of Judgment Day! I was siting off to the left and a little behind Tom, and as the tape played, his bald head just got redder and *redder.* He started protesting, but the more he protested, the more you could identify the voice on the tape!

"The wicked are trapped by their own words..."
(Proverbs 12:13 GNB)

"...I will use your own words to condemn you!..."
(Luke 19:22 GNB)

He was bragging about how he had drugged Micah and hired a makeup artist to paint cuts and bruises on his body. He boasted about beating *me* up, and then he started mocking the judge!

"The (blankety-blank) judge bought the whole thing hook line and sinker!"

Jeanette: The judge pressed pause and looked at Tom. He pressed rewind. Stop. And then played it again, all the time glaring at Tom with a look that said, *"You have had it!"*

Tom stood up and said, "I take it all back! I resign from this!" But the judge said, *"Oh no!"* and had him arrested right then and there.

He was convicted of purgery and submitting false evidence to the court.

He was in jail for six months.

And he lost visitation rights for two years.

When we got Micah back, he seemed groggy, like he had been sedated.

We learned later, that Tom had his truck packed and was ready to go. He and Micah had gotten their shots. They had their passports and their plane tickets. They were leaving the country— that day.

If that woman hadn't done what she did, we probably never would have seen Micah again.

Avis knew Tom was a dangerous man; she'd heard the stories, and normally she would have avoided him. But when he started boasting at work about what he was doing to his ex-wife ("I can just see DHS going into her house and pulling her nursing baby out of her arms as she screams...") she knew she had to do something.

She called the Ventura County Courthouse to check if there really was a hearing. There was. So she feigned interest in Tom, invited him to her house, and offered him wine. Before the night was over, she had his full confession on tape.

She drove five hours to get to the courthouse.

She was scared to death because she was certain Tom would try to take revenge. (And he did.) Yet she willingly put herself in harm's way— to help total strangers— from the other side of the country.

Even our lawyer thought this was divine intervention. He'd never seen anything like it.

Ken:

Life is full of all kinds of injustices and unfair deals, but if people will just stop and invite the God of the universe into their lives, justice will be served. Sometimes it's on the other side of suffering, but justice *will* be served.

"For God shall bring every work into judgment, with every secret thing, whether it be good, or whether it be evil."
(Ecclesiastes 12:14 KJV)

And don't ever give in to your anger. The Lord *will* take care of things.

"Deliver my soul, O LORD, from lying lips, and from a deceitful tongue."
(Psalm 120:2 KJV)

"Dearly beloved, avenge not yourselves but rather give place unto wrath: for it is written, Vengeance is mine; I will repay, saith the Lord."
(Romans 12:19 KJV)

Distance

Ruthie's Story

I was raised in a Christian home, but as a young married woman I found myself living a very sinful life, far from the Lord. Yet although I was keeping God at a distance, He was seeking to close the gap between us.

One day after work, I was walking in front of my office when I noticed a man up the street walking in my direction. The moment I saw him, I started rushing to get to my car. I don't know why; I'd never seen the man before, and he didn't look in the least bit threatening. —But something in my heart told me to get away from him.

"Everyone who does evil hates the light, and will not come into the light for fear that his deeds will be exposed."
(John 3:20-21 NIV)

He was at least a hundred yards up the street, and I was only twenty-five feet from my car, but when I opened the door and turned to sit, he was there, right in front of me.

As I stared at him, he calmly asked, "Are you walking with the Lord?"

I snapped at him. "No! I'm *running* with the Lord!"

"Are you sure?" he asked very gently.

"*Yes!*" I said, and jumped into my car and slammed the door. But when I looked up, he was gone. I looked all around; he was nowhere to be seen.

At first I just thought it was weird that a stranger would come up and ask me about God, but when I talked to my husband about the incident, I began to realize that he couldn't have been an ordinary man. There was no way he could have traveled the distance of a hundred yards in a few seconds, and it was impossible for him to vanish the way he did; there was nowhere for him to hide. The whole thing really shook me up and as we talked it over, we both began to believe, he must have been an angel.

After this incident, I tried to fix myself. I did what I'd been trained my whole life to do. I started reading my Bible, I started praying, and I started going to church. —But eventually I came to a place where I realized, *I couldn't* fix myself and I cried out to the Lord. "God, if you can't fix me then I can't be fixed!"

The Lord was right there waiting for me. He forgave my sin and I was filled with overwhelming joy and peace I didn't know were possible. I became, what the Bible calls, a *new creation*, and I was able to walk away from my sin.

By studying His word and walking closely with Him, The Lord changed my life completely. He restored my marriage, renewed my love for my family, and has given me more blessings than I can count.

And I now understand, that no matter how much distance I thought was between myself and the Lord, He was right there beside me all the time.

"...For God has said,
I will never leave you;
I will never abandon you."
(Hebrews 13:5 GNB)

The Hiding Place

Herb and Flo's Story

It is a pleasure to report
on God's blessing of yesterday,
how He supplied a need.

We moved to Houston, Texas, my wife Flo and I, in order that I might minister on behalf of Teen Challenge. For four years I was the director of Houston Teen Challenge. And you have to understand, I didn't make a lot. Flo and I learned to live on practically nothing. Then it became time, because of age and other things, for me to resign and head back up to Springfield, Missouri.

We put our home up for sale, a nice house on a beautiful corner. But it didn't sell. For almost two months it didn't sell, and we couldn't understand it. Other houses in our area were selling in two to three weeks. But there were *absolutely* no buyers for our house. No one even looked at it.

We had around $19,000.00 in credit card bills and such, so we waited on the Lord to provide, and I went to work. I started working for a church, painting and doing carpentry work and so forth. And still the house didn't sell. So I told my wife, “Honey, take it easy. Don't pack too much, because we may still be here in the fall.”

Then one day I received a telephone call from my wife. She said, “Honey. You'd better sit down for what I've got to tell you. You know that door near the sink in the kitchen, the long thin one where I keep my cookie tins and such?”

I said, “Yes.”

"Well, I pulled all the tins out, and I pulled out all the dividers. I reached way in back to wipe down the shelf, and something came loose. It was a pink rag, and when I pulled it out, I found a roll of money..."

I said, "Go on."

"I pulled out the bottom drawer next to that cabinet— and found *another* roll of money. —Honey, I just found twenty-*thousand* dollars!"

Naturally I went home.

I had to go see the provision God had made.

And wouldn't you know, the very next Saturday, the house sold.

With the help of that $20,000.00, we were able to leave Houston debt free. I paid off my $10,000.00 credit card for Teen Challenge; paid another bill for $9,000.00; tithed; and rented three U-Haul trucks to haul all of our stuff back up to Springfield. Once there, we found a house on foreclosure, and bought it outright.

It was an unusual provision of God's grace and love.

And one more thing. When we bought our nice house on that beautiful corner in Houston, it had been sitting on the market for three *years.*

Houses in that area generally sold in two to three *weeks.*

Whatever your experience may be,
you have a God who is just beyond that.
He is beyond the length of your problem.
No matter how much you may feel in the mullygrubs,
as they say down in Texas, that is not the end.
God is just beyond.

"O the depth of the riches
both of the wisdom and knowledge of God!
How unsearchable are his judgments,
and his ways past finding out!"
(Romans 11:33 KJV)

Teen Challenge is a Biblically based organization for drug addicts and alcoholics, which claims a 70-86% cure rate. Studies have supported this claim. In one study, 80% of the respondents credited developing a personal relationship with Jesus Christ as a major influence in helping them to stay off drugs.

Visit their web site at
www.teenchallengeusa.com,
or go to
http:/n.wikipedia.org
wikiTeen_Challenge
for more study results.

The Sobering Truth

Bob's Story

And as I lay there staring out into that all consuming, complete and total darkness, I heard a voice, and it said, ***"This is what it's like without me."***

As a third grader I began my football career. I loved the game, I was good at it, and the coaches took a shine to me. For three years, I played and was a happy kid— but then my little sister got very sick. She was born with cystic fibrosis and at the age of eight, the disease attacked her body with a vengeance, and we lost her. This threw my family into an awful turmoil, and my parents split up.

My older brother turned to drugs, and at the age of twelve, I started drinking. When football season came around, I threw my heart and soul into the game. It gave me a sense of purpose, and it helped me forget my troubles, but when the season ended, I was empty. So as a sixth grader, I dove head first into the world of drugs. First my big brother introduced me to marijuana, then it was PCP, then mescaline, then opium.

I missed my eighth grade graduation because of an overdose, and in high school, I had to pick my big brother up off the playground in front of everyone because he was passed out drunk. I was never more ashamed or embarrassed in my life, and I knew I needed to get away from that lifestyle. So I focused harder on football. But each year when football season was over, I found myself with a lot of time on my hands.

I wanted to get away from drugs, but I needed something to fill the void. Then in my sophomore year, my coach hooked me up with a weight lifting program, and every day after school, I was in the weight room, working as hard as I could.

On New Years Eve when I was fifteen years old, I told my brother I wasn't going to do drugs anymore. He laughed because he didn't think I could do it. But I did do it. I forsook everything and focused on football and football alone. I wanted to be the best football player there ever was, and for the next two years, I kept my nose clean, I worked as hard as I could, and I made the All State team.

When Syracuse University offered me a full scholarship, I took it. But as soon as I got there, I began to struggle. An offensive lineman was supposed to weigh 250 pounds or more— but no matter how many grueling hours I spent in the weight room, or how much I ate, I couldn't gain enough muscle mass to push me over two-fifty. And if I didn't gain the weight, I would never make it to the pros. I was also struggling academically, so when I was given the opportunity to transfer to a smaller school closer to home, I took it.

I was more comfortable there, but as soon as I walked into the locker room, my eyes were opened to what was going on. The use of steroids was rampant! At first I was shocked, but the more I thought about it, the more I thought I'd found the answer to my problem. If I took this drug, I could gain the weight I needed, and if I gained the weight, I could make it to the pros. —I had told my brother I wasn't going to do drugs anymore— but this was something different.

I started taking steroids and started increasing in size and strength. I got my weight up over two-fifty and was playing better than ever. So when I read about the potential side effects, I paid no attention.

Among other things, anabolic steroid use in men can cause emotional problems, violent anger, accelerated baldness, impotence, trembling, swollen feet and ankles, jaundice, halitosis, aching joints, high blood pressure, kidney and blood disorders, liver damage, and cancer.

During summer breaks, I worked as a camp counselor for the recreation department, and the summer before my senior year, I took a group of kids on a field trip to see the New England Patriots.

Then during my senior year at Rhode Island, I played so well, that I made First Team All Conference, and two NFL teams began recruiting me. I was tempted to go with the Dallas Cowboys, but ultimately chose the New England Patriots.

When I arrived in Foxboro, I was still on steroids and fit right in in terms of size and strength. I was given a trial as a free agent and one day I got a little taste of what it would be like to be famous. I was walking off the field with John Hannah, an All Pro and now a Hall of Fame offensive lineman, when all of a sudden a large group of kids came running up to us. But they didn't want John's autograph, they wanted mine! Because they were my kids from the recreation department— and I was loving every minute of it!

For awhile it looked like I had a pretty good shot at making the team. I fit right in, I was playing well, and with my combined three lifts, I was the strongest rookie in the camp. But then I started to realize, I was just a tad bit slower than some of the other guys— and then I hurt my ankle.

The day I got cut from the Patriots was in late August and I remember it well. Dick Steinburg called me into his office and told me I could definitely fit into the league— but the Patriots simply didn't have room for me. I felt like somebody had died. It was the death of my vision, the death of my hope. —So I went out and got as drunk as I could. It was the only way I knew to kill the pain.

Then I got a call from a USFL team in Houston. They sent me airline tickets, but before I flew down for the tryouts, I was brought to see a prestigious doctor in a major Rhode Island hospital. Because I was a local hero, he was going to supply me with steroids. He called it a "necessary evil."

In Houston, steroid use was the worst I'd seen. Guys were walking around with bags of drugs in plain sight, and shooting up in the locker room in front of everyone. I had always tried to hide the steroids, but these guys had no problem flaunting their "necessary evil."

I started trying out for the team and was making it to every practice, but then afterwards, I would go back to the hotel and get drunk. Parties were ongoing, the night clubs let us in free, and people were always buying us food and drinks. At first, I thought this was awesome, but as time went on I realized, if I stayed in football, I was going to end up seriously messed up— or dead. So I started praying every morning, "Lord give me the strength to keep on going, the wisdom to know right from wrong, and the courage to do the right thing." It was like a mantra, and I didn't really understand what I was saying, yet God was answering that prayer.

One night at a team meeting, I was sitting there

totally ripped from the drinks I'd consumed with dinner, when one of the guys stood up and announced there was going to be a Bible study on Thursday nights. A *Bible* study? That was an interesting concept. I didn't even know what a Bible study was. This guy was a respected player, the captain of the defense, and he'd received All League Honors the year before. This guy seemed to have his life together, and I remember looking down at my hands and thinking, *My* life is a *mess.*

One morning soon after this, I found myself looking in the mirror, and all I could say was, "God get me out of here! I can't do this anymore." I had a twenty-two inch neck. I could squat close to seven hundred pounds, and I was benching about four hundred.

I was a mass of strength— but I was an empty shell.

This time when I got called into the office for the bad news, I was okay. At the previous practice, I remember having my helmet on and thinking, *This is the last time I'm going to wear this thing.* I knew it was final. I'd had enough.

Soon after this, a friend hooked me up with a job in Maine as a teacher and a coach at Bangor High School. I had vowed to myself when I was cut from the team in Houston that I wouldn't take steroids anymore, but I forgot one thing. I forgot I had to go through withdrawals. The doctor said it could take up to five years to get over withdrawals. It took me a year.

Trying to adjust to a new job in a new state while going through steroid withdrawals was not easy. I felt washed out, weak, exhausted, and barely human. I lost sixty-six pounds in seven months and I had a hard time controlling my anger. One day a student mouthed off to me in the gym and I shoved him hard through a curtain divider.

I almost lost my job over this.

During this time I met and married my wife, Stephanie, and we had two boys. At one point, we went to visit my mom and dad in Rhode Island and we stopped in to see my old high school coach, Dennis O'Brien. He had always been like a second father to me, so when I heard he was diagnosed with terminal heart disease, I was anxious to see him.

During our visit, I could tell that something was very different about him. He was an Irish Catholic who had always been very committed— committed to smoking and drinking. I expected him to offer me a drink, but he didn't. Instead, he looked at me from his chair and said, "Bob, the best thing you can ever know is in this book." He was talking about the Bible, and he told me that he and his wife had started going to a Bible study. *A Bible study.* Again I was intrigued.

Dennis had stopped drinking, but for me, even though I had never gone back to drugs after the steroids, drinking was a different story. I started drinking when I was twelve years old, and after twenty years, it was still the only way I knew how to cope. Then when my brother died of an overdose in 1989, and my father died of leukemia in 1990, my drinking accelerated.

After these events and a football coaching job that went sour, I got a job coaching with a man who was a Green Beret in Viet Nam, and when there was time after practice, or on the bus, Don shared his story with me. He told about his experience in the war, and how he had come back a total mess, but that the Lord had saved him.

He was supposed to resign from coaching and move out of state, but decided to stay on for one more year. And when my anger once again landed me on the hot seat, he stood up for me and said, "I believe the Lord wanted me to stay coaching one more year for Bob. The only reason I'm here is for Bob."

I was blown away! I didn't know what he was talking about! But he got me off the hook. —Then he invited me to a Bible study.

After several invites, I decided to go.

They were studying in the book of Romans, and as I sat listening, the verses began to grip my heart. I was a sinner, and I deserved to go to hell. I immediately started thinking, *Where can I go? There's no where to hide, God is going to judge me.* But as I continued to listen, I learned how to receive forgiveness through Jesus who died for me, and I prayed for forgiveness.

Immediately I began to notice a change in myself. During this period of my life I had been pursuing another love of mine, music. I'd been playing in a band for several years, and all of a sudden some of the words in our songs became offensive and I didn't want to sing them anymore. God was changing me, but everything didn't change at once. I was still drinking. For three years, I drank at least a six pack every day and went through one or two bottles of Jack Daniels a week. If we went somewhere where alcohol was not allowed, I hid a bottle in my pocket and drank it in the bathroom.

One night at another Bible study, another scripture gripped me. It's in Ephesians and it says, "Don't be drunk with wine, but be filled with the Holy Spirit." This really got my attention, and I asked the guys to pray for me. I knew I needed to stop drinking and I wasn't sure if I could do it on my own. They prayed for me, and I stopped, for awhile. Then I went on a hunting trip with my in-laws.

I got back to the camp before anyone else and

noticed a bottle of gin sitting on the shelf. I thought to myself, *I can have just one drink.* But then something snapped. I finished the bottle and stole my brother in-law's truck to go get more. That's all I remember.

They came and got me because they heard rounds being shot off in the woods. I don't remember the ride home but I remember my wife. She was *livid.* She had been at the end of her rope for some time, and I didn't even know it! She took one look at me, took the kids, and left.

I vaguely remember going downstairs to the kids room, lying on the bottom bunk, having bed spins, and falling asleep.

When I woke up, I was in total darkness, and I knew I had a problem. My wife and kids were gone, and I couldn't stop drinking. For years I'd looked down on my brother because he was addicted to drugs, but there in the darkness, I realized for the first time, that I was just as bad as he had been. I wanted to stop drinking, but now I knew I couldn't do it on my own.

And as I lay there staring out into that all consuming, complete and total darkness, I heard a voice, and it said, *"This is what it's like without me."*

I cried. "I can't do it. —I don't want this. —I don't want darkness. —*I can't do this Lord! I need your help! I can't stop drinking! Please help me!"*

After that night, I never had another drink. The Lord cured me. Right then and there I was healed— and I vowed in my heart that I would serve Him.

"and call upon me in the day of trouble; I will deliver you, and you shall glorify me."
(Psalm 50:15 ESV)

There was a time when I sought fame because I thought it would satisfy. But today I know that recognition is simply knowing that you are God's son or daughter. There was a time when I thought physical strength was the answer, but now I know that real strength can only come from the Lord.

"For bodily exercise profits a little,
but godliness is profitable to all things,
having promise of the present life,
and of that which is to come."
(1 Timothy 4:8 MKJV)

Because of my use of steroids, my joints are in very bad shape. A couple of years ago, I had an MRI and the doctor said I have the knees of an eighty-five year old man. The cartilage is almost touching. It's almost bone on bone. This is not normal for a forty-three year old. A friend of mine from college played in the NFL for six years and was on steroids much longer than I was. He died at 38 from heart disease.

My advice to young people is to trust in the Lord, not in your own strength. Let God guide and direct you. When you have to train for something, give it all you've got, but give it over to God, and if it is His will for your life, He'll give it to you.

Any time I have difficulty, I go back to that day I cried out in the darkness. I learned something that night that I will never forget. No matter how complete the darkness, it cannot extinguish the light. And the only thing that can take away spiritual darkness, is *The* Light.

"And cast ye the
unprofitable servant into
outer darkness: there shall be weeping
and gnashing of teeth."
(Matthew 25:30 KJV)

"Then Jesus spoke again
to them, saying, I am the Light
of the world. He who follows Me
shall not walk in darkness..."
(John 8:12 MKJV)

Little Warrior

Eryn's Story

I saw a picture of my baby today. So far he just looks like a little blob, but I'm in love already. The doctor says everything looks good, and if the baby arrives on schedule, it will be born on April 13, 2004. Brian and I are happy, and Orianna is excited about having a baby brother or sister to play with. I've been having weird pains, but the doctor says it's nothing to worry about.

I'm about half way to my due date and the baby's kicking a lot now. Orianna is so funny. Every day she comes up to me and wraps her arms around my belly. First she kisses it on one side, then on the other, and then in the middle. It's the cutest thing. She can hardly wait to meet the baby.

I'm worried because the pain I've been having since I got pregnant hasn't gone away like everyone said it would. I'm twenty-five weeks along and I still have bad cramps every day. It's bearable, but it worries me. I want to have another ultrasound to make sure the baby's okay, but since my first pregnancy was normal, and my insurance won't cover another ultrasound, the doctor sees no reason for it.

We still don't know if we're having a boy or a girl. Brian wants to know but I want to be surprised. And we haven't agreed on a name if it's a boy. If it's a girl, we'll name her Evangelina, after Brian's grandmother, but I don't feel at peace with it being a girl. I believe this baby is a little boy, and I want to name him Jeshua, but Brian doesn't like it, and he's hated every other name I've suggested.

I'm six weeks away from the baby's due date. The pain has never fully gone away and we still can't agree on a boy's name. Today I looked through a book of baby names and still didn't find anything, but when I put the book down, the name Wyatt popped into my head. It sounds perfect to me, but I know Brian will hate it, so I won't say anything.

Yesterday I thought of the name Wyatt, and this morning, before Brian's feet even hit the floor, he said to me, "Honey, what do you think of the name Wyatt?" Now I'm sure we're having a boy, because the Lord has given us his name. I'd like to find out what it means.

Brian's son Noah is hoping the baby will be born on his birthday, which is March, 30th. I keep telling him the baby is due April 13th and there is no *way* I am going to have him two weeks early. But he keeps bugging me about it. He wants us to name the baby after him if it's a boy and if he's born on his birthday. I told him not to hold his breath.

I'm over eight months pregnant and the doctor says the baby should have turned by now. He should be pointing downward, but I can feel his head constantly pressing up underneath my rib cage. It's *very* uncomfortable. No matter what position I get into, it still hurts. The doctor finally scheduled another ultrasound. I'll go in on Thursday, March 26th.

It was exciting to see the picture of the baby. Those

machines are just the coolest things. Orianna came in with us and her eyes lit up when she saw the baby on the screen. After having the ultrasound, Brian went out into the hallway to talk to the technician. I think he was asking about the sex of the baby. We've waited this long! Can't he wait a couple more weeks? Besides, I know I am having a boy— and I can't wait to meet him.

—We are completely devastated. —I don't know which way is up. My doctor told us the reason the baby hasn't turned is because he has something called hydrocephalus. I've never even heard that word before! I don't know what to think! The doctor said something about his head being too large because of water on the brain and that something might be wrong with his heart! It's possible he might not live very long. He's going to send me to a specialist on Tuesday. We've finally stopped crying enough to get on the phone and ask people to pray. Brian is talking to Justin Alfred in California right now ...

We stayed up almost all night praying and calling people. I might have slept for an hour or two. I woke up at 3:00 and heard Brian say, "Lord, if you wanted to get my attention, you've got it!" I don't think he slept at all. Last night we got on line and looked up hydrocephalus. One site had this awful picture of a little baby with a huge disfigured head. It looked like an alien! I can't shake the image from my mind. I wish we hadn't looked at it! My head is swimming and I just don't know what to do. Orianna keeps asking us what's wrong, but we don't know what to tell her.

We've called everyone we can think of and asked them to pray for the baby. I haven't slept much in the last couple of days and I'm supposed to go in to see the specialist tomorrow to get a better idea of what's going on. —Despite everything, I know God is in control.

It is a few hours later and I just got off the phone with my doctor. It's even worse than we thought. He reviewed the ultrasound and they can't find one of the baby's kidneys! He doesn't know if staying inside the womb is good or bad for him. I have no idea what we're facing. —I might give birth to a dead baby. —I just don't know. —The waiting is killing me.

It's March 30th and I'm heading to the hospital to see the specialist. I'm very tired but I know the Lord is with us. I know a lot of people are praying.

They did another ultrasound at 10:30 and we waited until noon to hear the results. The specialist said the baby has the worst case of hydrocephalus he has ever seen and he doesn't know how long he'll live. —He said it could be a couple of hours, or maybe as long as a couple of months. They want to do an amniocentesis on me. They're going to stick a needle through my abdomen and take out some of the amniotic fluid to check it. I'm scared to do it— but I'll do anything if it will help the baby.

They want to do the amnio at 2:30 so I'm home making calls for Orianna to be picked up from school. I called her and told her I love her and that she might spend the night with her friend because Mommy has to go for a test in the hospital. She was okay with that. She's been amazingly good these last few days considering the circumstances. It's hard to believe she's only six. We're going to have a quick prayer and then we have to head straight back to the hospital.

It looks like this baby isn't going to wait two more weeks to be born. When we got here they brought us right up to labor and delivery and by four o'clock they finished the amniocentesis. It was horrible! I don't want to do *that* again! I've started having contractions and they have me hooked up to a monitor to see how strong they are. They're starting to get worse so I probably won't be able to write for a while.

It's the next day and I'm still in shock. Yesterday at 5:30 my contractions were getting worse and the doctor came in and said they were going to go ahead and deliver the baby. I asked him when, and he said, "*Right now*." It all happened so fast. I didn't have time to do anything, except pray. At 6:00 they said they were going to deliver him, at 6:15 they brought in blues for Brian, at 6:30 they prepped me for the caesarian, and at 7:11 Wyatt was born.

I'm in a lot of pain. I hurt all over. Everything happened *so* fast. It's all just a blur. They cleaned him up and I heard him cry once. He was wrapped up tight in a blanket and I only got to see him for a minute. He has the sweetest little face I have ever seen. He was all pink and cute and then they whisked him away to the Neonatal Intensive Care Unit. I didn't even get to hold him. Later on they wheeled my bed into the NICU so I could see him. It was so hard not to be able to just pick up my baby and hold him.

I've had no time to prepare for all of this. I thought I

was going to have a baby two weeks from now on April 13th, but I ended up having him on March 30th, Noah's birthday! He was right after all. I asked Brian if we could name the baby Wyatt Jeshua and he said, "Well we have to put Noah in there too." So his name is Wyatt Jeshua Noah. Now Brian has two sons born on the same day, twenty-one years apart.

Today Wyatt is one day old and they let me hold him. He weighs seven pounds four ounces and is seventeen and a half inches long. His head is larger than normal but I think he's just perfect. He's so cute! They want to do a shunt operation on him tomorrow. They will put a tube inside his body from his head to his abdomen to drain the fluid off his brain. We're praying he won't suffer and that the operation will be a success. I'm still exhausted and in a tremendous amount of pain, but I am focused on Wyatt. I've tried nursing him but he just isn't into it. The Lactation Consultant came in and tried to help me but I kicked her out. I know what I'm doing. I nursed Orianna without any problems. If Wyatt is going to nurse, he'll nurse, otherwise, we'll just enjoy being close and I'll pump my milk so he can have it anyway.

The neurosurgeon came in to talk to us about the shunt surgery, but what he said wasn't matching up with what the doctor told us earlier. When he saw we were confused he said, "Don't you know?" And we said, "Don't we know *what?*" He was irritated and went out and told our doctor he needed to tell us what was going on. Then we were told Wyatt has something called holoprosencephaly. He said that only half of Wyatt's brain formed and basically, Wyatt doesn't have a brain! He said Wyatt may never do anything, that he may be a vegetable for as long as he lives! They didn't give us any hope. But I'm not ready to give up. —God can do anything!

We just found a verse in Romans that gives us hope. The doctor said Wyatt doesn't have a brain. Well, God can fix it if he wants to. Romans 4:17 says "... This happened because Abraham believed in the God who brings the dead back to life and who brings into existence what didn't exist before." If God wants to make Wyatt whole, he can do it.

It's Thursday morning and Wyatt is two days old. I went in and held him and prayed. I want God's will to be done, whatever that might be, but I don't want to lose him! My friend called last night and said Pastor Ken told the congregation about Wyatt and that they prayed for us. Ken came in just after Wyatt was born and prayed with us too. People have already started showing up with cards and words of encouragement. I know the Lord is in control. He can do anything. If he wants to heal Wyatt, he will heal Wyatt, if not, then we will take it one day at a time.

Several people have joined us for prayer while the surgery is going on. They will cut a hole in Wyatt's head, and string a tube under his skin from his head down to his abdomen where the fluid will drain and be absorbed into his body. One of the nurses printed some information about holoprosencephaly. These words are so foreign to me. I hope Wyatt isn't in any pain. He's so tiny. Lord Jesus please let him be okay.

They had to stop the surgery. Apparently Wyatt has pulmonary hypertension which means that his oxygen and heart rate are unstable. When they gave him the anesthesia, he couldn't handle it and his lungs filled up with fluid. They put a tube down his throat so he could breathe but when they took it out, he was struggling so hard that they had to "re-intubate" him, they had to put the tube back down his throat. So now he's worse off than before.

He didn't do well over the weekend. At the team meeting, they didn't come right out and say it but they were asking us if we wanted to let him go, to stop treatment and just let him die! *They've* given up on him already! Well *I* won't give up! I said, "If you're asking me to pull the plug, I'm not God and I don't have that choice!" I can't *believe* they would even ask us that!

Wyatt opened his eyes for the first time in three days. The trauma to his body and the medication put him out for awhile but he's doing better today.

Lord Jesus, I lift this baby up to you and I thank you for blessing me with this precious little boy. I love you so much and I know you love Wyatt more than I possibly ever could. I know you have a divine plan and I know your ways are not my ways nor are my thoughts your thoughts. Father, I pray for a tremendous miracle if it be your will. Just creating Wyatt has been a miracle. Now I'm begging that you would heal him.

Wyatt is six days old and they need to discharge me, but they're letting me stay in the room until they need it for someone else. I'm glad because I can't imagine leaving Wyatt alone. He still has the breathing tube down his throat and a feeding tube in his nose. I'm still pumping so he can have mother's milk.

Today the doctor told me they're going to do the shunt surgery again on Monday, April 12th. And the social worker told me they need my room. They gave me an hour's notice. So I packed up my things, brought everything home, and came right back again. I'm feeling very stressed right now, very tense, and I'm praying for peace. When the social worker told me they needed the room, it scared me and I thought maybe they were just doing it because they don't want me around any more. Oh God please take this anxiety away from me.

Today is April 13th, Wyatt's due date, but instead he is two weeks old. Yesterday they did the shunt surgery and it was a success! A bunch of people from church came to pray with us and the hospital let us use one of the conference rooms which was nice. He seems to be doing well. He's resting comfortably.

I'm happy to have another day with my sweet little guy. Linda, one of Wyatt's nurses asked me if I'd like to get some hand and foot prints. I said, "YES! What a great idea!" We made some prints on paper and put some in the front cover of my prayer journal. They came out really nice. You can even see the imprint of the Band Aids on his tiny heels. He has the cutest little feet in the whole world!

It's two days after the surgery and Wyatt's shunt is slipping out. They have to operate *again*. This is very frustrating. I just want Wyatt stabilized so I can bring him home, this is my constant prayer. I will do whatever it takes to bring him home.

I held Wyatt for four hours straight today. The nurses said, “Why don’t you go home and take a break?” But I told them no. I just wanted to keep looking at his beautiful little face. He has my nose and ears and maybe my mouth. He has his father’s toes and fingers. He is a combination of the two of us and I just love him. I feel totally blessed to be the mother of this little baby boy. I pray God will mold me into the mother he wants me to be.

They fixed the shunt. Jeanette and a few others came in and sat with me during the operation. The doctor said it looks good. We’ll see.

They did another CT scan and it still wasn’t working. It was still poking out! So they went in again and this time they finally got it right. I’m getting frustrated with the doctors. —But I need to just give it over to God. *He* is in control and I need to stop and pray and know that even though I don’t understand why all this is happening, he will get me through it.

Today was a good day. Wyatt’s doing well and I have a free cel phone! I told Tonya it was hard to get errands done because when I go home, I want to stay right at the house in case the hospital calls. Tonya told her coworkers at Unicel about me and they all wanted to help. They passed the hat and today she brought in a gift basket, some money and a free cel phone! What a blessing!

Wyatt’s shunt is working, but because of the pressure in his head, he’s starting to have seizures and they put him on Phenobarbital. He’s had the breathing tube for two weeks now and they’re going to take it out to see if he can breathe on his own. If he can do it, we will be one step closer to going home.

I am so mad right now, I could just …! It was time for rounds so Dad and I had to leave. I knew they were planning on extubating Wyatt at some point and I talked to Wyatt's doctor and told him I did *not* want Wyatt to suffer. I told him if Wyatt couldn't breathe on his own I wanted him to be reintubated *right away*. He said he'd pass it along to the doctor coming on the next shift, but he didn't! Dad and I were sitting outside the maternity ward waiting for rounds to be over when a nurse came out and said they were looking for me. When we went in, Wyatt was doing awful! He couldn't breathe! His eyes were big and black and his skin was gray! It looked like he'd been struggling for a *long* time! The doctor wanted to know what I wanted to do! No one had told her anything! I told her I could stand there all night trying to comfort him but I wasn't going to. I said, "Get that tube in his mouth NOW! I don't want to wait!" And I walked out! They didn't need to let him suffer! They could easily have found me! They had my cel phone number! They could have paged me in the hospital! I don't ever want to see my baby like that again! There was absolutely no need for that!

It's Thursday, April 22nd and Wyatt is three weeks old. They did another MRI and now the doctor tells us Wyatt *doesn't* have holoprosencephaly but that he has something called an absent corpus callosum. They think the messenger box that allows the two sides of his brain to communicate is *missing*. So they said, sorry we made you learn about holoprosencephaly, he doesn't have it, he has this other thing. —I am *not* gaining any confidence in these people.

We had another team meeting today. I asked if it would be possible for Wyatt to have a tracheostomy, a permanent breathing tube in his neck. One of the doctors said he would NEVER be a candidate for a trache. He said it was not an option. So I let the matter drop, but I haven't given up on the idea.

I am so mortified right now! One of the nurses in the NICU told me if I wanted to, they could just give Wyatt some medicine and "let him go quietly."! I said, "How could you even say that to me! I'm NOT going to do *that!*" Then she asked me what his quality of life would be! I still can't believe she said that! I don't even want her touching Wyatt! Obviously she's done! It seems like no matter what we tell them, it's never a good enough answer. We are going to do what it takes to bring Wyatt home and give him the best life possible! The hospital wants us to pull the plug. I know they do! They say they're on our side and that they support us, but then they keep questioning us! What do you want to do? What do you want to do? WE WANT TO DO WHATEVER IT TAKES TO GET THIS BABY HOME! When the Lord is ready to take Wyatt, he'll take him, but it's not up to us to decide.

This morning I came across a verse in my Bible. It's Second Chronicles 20:12 and it says, "For we have no power against this great multitude that is coming against us; nor do we know what to do, but our eyes are upon you." That is what I am focusing on right now. No matter what happens or who may be against us, my eyes are focused on the Lord. He is in control, not the hospital.

Wyatt's primary day nurse is a good woman. She's honest with us and makes sure we know exactly what's going on, but she's also supportive. Today she confided in me and told me about a little boy like Wyatt, only his parents couldn't handle it and they abandoned him! His name was Alex and all of the nurses took him in as their own. A foster mother was found for him and she loved him but he never made it out of the hospital. He never got off the ventilator and he died. I can't stop thinking about him. How could a parent ever abandon their baby? I've been looking at the other moms in the hospital and I don't know how they do it without the Lord. I know the only reason I can do this is because the Lord is right here with me.

I've been told they're going to try one more time to extubate Wyatt, and if he isn't able to breathe on his own, they're sending us to Boston. There's nothing else they can do here.

Today is Friday, May 7th. Wyatt is five and a half weeks old. He went for ten hours today without the breathing tube with no luck. I held his hand and sang to him all day and he tried so hard, but he just can't do it. We're going to try one more time on Sunday, and if it doesn't work, we're going Boston.

Well Wyatt didn't wait until Sunday. He pulled the tube out all by himself on Saturday. He went for several hours without it and didn't do any better than the first time, so we'll be heading out on the 11th. And guess what he's going down for? A tracheostomy, the thing they said he would NEVER be a candidate for.

It's Tuesday, May 11th and I'm on my way to Boston. We left at 1:30 in the morning and we're almost there. They won't let me ride in the ambulance so a bunch of my friends offered to take me down. It's been a quiet ride. I talked for a little while to Holly, but Jen, Sarah, and Marcy are trying to sleep. We're not supposed to follow the ambulance but they stopped at the same rest stop, and we've passed each other a few times. We should arrive at about the same time. I don't understand why they wouldn't let me ride in the ambulance. This is stupid.

Back home, one of Wyatt's doctors said if Wyatt got a trache, he would still be on the ventilator and would have to live the rest of his life in the hospital. Well, Wyatt had his tracheostomy and guess what? A half an hour later, he was taken off the ventilator and he hasn't needed to go back on it! I am so proud of him! I thank God for each breath he takes.

BREATH

As a breath finally escapes from his small smooth mouth
The mist of the breath is in the air

As I breathe in
I wonder

Am I tasting a bit of his breath
Which is now becoming my own?

It seems so simple, breath
Like something so uncomplicated

But to a baby who is taking his first
It can seem so miraculous

So when you go to take your next
Remember that if it weren't so,
Neither would you be so

He's only been in this world for seven weeks and among other things, Wyatt has had four shunt surgeries, a tracheostomy, two MRIs, several CT scans, several x-rays, three EEGs, several echo grams, lots of ultrasounds and many, *many* kisses! At this hospital they are checking him out from head to toe.

Wyatt has NORMAL brain tissue!! The doctors tell me he has severe hydrocephalus but that he *doesn't* have holoprosencephaly *or* an absent corpus callosum. They think the fluid on his brain pushed his brain so far back against his skull that the doctors at home couldn't see it, but now they can see it! And it's *normal!* This is huge! The verse in Romans says God can bring into existence that which didn't exist before. That verse came true! They said he didn't have a brain, and now it's there! God can do anything!

The tracheostomy was a success. I'm happy about that, but now his shunt is ripping open and starting to poke through his head. I can see the white tube sticking out. They have to assume that it's contaminated and take the whole thing out. They're putting in a new one tonight. I'm praying this will be the last time. Since these doctors have more experience, I'm hoping they can figure out what's going wrong and make it right once and for all.

Well, it didn't get done and now it's the weekend. For some reason they can't do shunt operations on the weekend so they had to put him on an externalized drain. Now he has a tube that goes from his head to a bag next to his bed. He has to be kept at just the right level. If he's too high, it will drain too fast, and if he's too low, it will drain too slowly. On a positive note, he hasn't been having seizures.

It's Saturday, May 22nd. They gave Wyatt morphine and he stopped breathing *seven* times in the last 24 hours! Every time he stopped they had to bag him to get him breathing again. I don't *ever* want him to go through that again!

A week and a half has gone by. They said they were going to do the shunt on Monday. But on Monday we got bumped to Wednesday. And on Wednesday they said they couldn't do it until Friday! They keep thanking me for being so patient but I'm getting frustrated. The externalized drain is *highly* serious. There's a high risk of infection and it shouldn't be left in any longer than it absolutely has to be. He's supposed to go in for surgery on Wednesday, May 26th— *if* we don't get bumped again.

My nerves are right on edge. It is *so* loud in this hospital and I'm having a really hard time comforting Wyatt with all this noise going on. I don't know if he is in distress but he won't settle down and the noise is driving me crazy!

Dear Father, I pray that in a miraculous way you

would quiet the noise and let Wyatt hear only your music. The louder it gets the more upset I get. I need to pump and I need to know Wyatt will be okay if I leave for awhile. Lord I pray for all of these babies and their parents. I pray for baby Sarah, Matthew, Jacob, Joshua and this baby across from us who is always crying. You know his name. I don't know his name but I know he is fighting because I hear his pain. Please give us your peace. Please give us your comfort and quiet so that Wyatt will fall asleep and rest in your arms.

I've been talking to Brian and things aren't going well. He doesn't think it would be a good idea to bring the baby home. At first he was with me all the way but now he's having personal problems that need to be dealt with. He's going away for awhile and Orianna is going to stay with some friends...

So much is happening here and at home that sometimes my mind just can't take it anymore. But when I turn to prayer and God's word, he comforts me. Earlier while I was reading my Bible, I came across a verse in John. It says, "When Jesus heard that, he said, This sickness is not unto death, but for the glory of God, that the Son of God might be glorified thereby."

Voice inside my head
Question, thoughts of things people have said
My mind searches for answers
Wonders at why this could be

But the moment that I start that
Is when I stop being me

Me is the question of who I really am
The answer to that one is a Christian ‘til the end

The end is endless because of my faith
To know that I’ll be in heaven and not in this place
So while I am here and questioning the rules
My spirit reminds me of salvation and the tools,

Which are the reminders in each day that passes
To keep God in the center and the rest in the wings
To be present in the moment, focus on the things above
Never question, never turn from the one true love

I thank God for his passion and commitment to me
I thank God for his faithfulness and love overflowing
through me
I thank God for his strength and his mercy and his grace
I thank God for bringing me to this place

For showing me that his power is greater than any other
That he loves me and cares for me like no other
Thank him for the child that he has blessed me with
And the strength that he has given him to make it through
the day

I know that his plan is greater than I can fathom
And I know that his love larger than I can imagine
He gives life to this child and grace to him too
He is constantly pouring mercy on us through and through

I pray that his plan is one I can understand
But even if I don’t he will help to comprehend
That his purpose is for his glory

And that I can understand

Well Wyatt finally had the surgery they've been putting off, but instead of putting in a new shunt, they did an Endoscopic Third Ventriculostomy, which should allow him to be shunt free. They think he had Aqueductal Stenosis which means that the reservoir where the fluid drains out of the head into the spine was clogged. If the surgery is successful, then the fluid will drain naturally! That would be wonderful! I'm so glad these doctors are willing to go ahead and try different things to help Wyatt. The neurosurgeon even came and spoke to me personally to let me know the surgery went well. Praise the Lord.

Wyatt just had the worst seizure I have ever seen. It scared me and I hope it doesn't happen again. They did an eye and hearing test on him. He failed both tests. But what did they expect so soon after major surgery? Before the surgery, when they flashed a light in his eyes he would squint, but now he doesn't, and it seems like a part of him is gone.

Today Evelyn came to visit me from Calvary Chapel Fitchburg. What a wonderful friend! She brought a great big gift basket and some money from the church. I can use the money; everything is so expensive here. I don't know where I'd be without the church helping us out. Even people who don't know me from a hole in the wall want to help us. Pastor Steve from the Calvary Chapel in the city visited me last week and Pastor George Small from the Fitchburg church is supposed to be coming sometime. God is good.

Because of the externalized drain, it's been almost two weeks since I held Wyatt, but I come in every day and sit with him for hours. He has a private room now and they put a cot in here so I can cuddle up beside him. I hold his hand and stroke his head. Sometimes I sing or read or play his CDs. We have a Comfort CD and one with harp music. The nurses finally stopped telling me to take a break. They understand that I want to be in here.

It was so great to be able to hold my baby again! They took the externalized drain out of his head and I held him for four hours straight. But then he started to feel a little warm so I put him back in his bed and took his temperature. He had a fever of 101. They took some samples and they're going to do a CT scan.

He has what's called basilis meningitis. Somehow, bacteria got into his cerebrospinal fluid (CFS for short). They think the Ventriculostomy didn't work so the CFS isn't draining, but they can't put in a shunt until the infection is gone, so they have to put him back on the externalized drain. They've started him on intense antibiotics. They tried to put a catheter into his leg to administer the medication but it wasn't working so they had to put one directly into his heart. It's called a broviac line.

—It looks like we're going to be here awhile.

I've been running low on cash but the Lord has provided. Someone at home found out I needed money and put $80.00 in my account. I also found a piece of glass in my food and when the hospital found out about it they apologized and gave me a $50.00 gift certificate. I can use it in the cafeteria or coffee shops.

Wyatt's been lying on his left side for the last eighteen days because of the externalized shunt. He's been on antibiotics for several days but he *still* has the infection, and he's still having seizures. One of his nurses said it's important to keep them under control but then another one said it's okay to let them happen! I got a third opinion and was told they definitely need to be kept under control, so I made it clear I wanted *all* the staff told that Wyatt's seizures need to be kept under control. I don't want anyone letting Wyatt suffer when it can be stopped.

Dad and Orianna came for a visit. The social worker got us a room at the Beacon House and Jord came and we all went out to eat. Dad was happy because he had both of his kids together. I didn't like being so far away from Wyatt but it was great to see my family. Before they left we walked down to the swan boats and took a ride in one of them. Orianna *loved* that.

I want her to stay here at the hospital but they won't let her stay in the family room with me. HELLO! It's called the *family* room. They offered to set us up at the Beacon House and have Ori go into the daycare but I don't have the money, I don't know the day care providers, and what's the point if she can't be with me? Hopefully I won't be here much longer. If only Wyatt would stabilize enough to have the shunt put back in.

Wyatt's numbers have been off the charts! They still aren't stable but they're going to go ahead and put the shunt in. They don't want to wait any longer because of the risk of further infection with the externalized drain. They're going to operate today. We've been here for six weeks and I want to go home.

The surgery went well. If nothing else happens, we're going home in one week. This time they're going to let me ride in the ambulance.

Wyatt is stable and we're going home tomorrow! I got to spend some more time with my brother today. I've only seen him a couple of times in the last two years so it's been good to see him. He came down and we drove over near the North end and walked along the water and had dinner together. I'm happy I got the chance to reconnect with him, but I'll be happier to get home!

We're on our way home! I don't get to ride in the back but the nurse taking care of Wyatt is a good one and he's worked with him before. I almost can't believe we are finally going home. We spent *seven* weeks in Boston! It was only supposed to be a few days. I can't wait to see everyone. It will be so good to be home!

I didn't tell Orianna we were coming home because I wanted to surprise her. Tonya met us at the hospital Wyatt's bed was decorated with balloons and welcome home signs. That was really nice. Then we went to Kelly and Garth's and I snuck upstairs to where Orianna was. I poked my head in the door and she just kind of looked at me and said, "Mommy?" Then she ran and threw her arms around me and didn't want to let go. She was *very* surprised. It was cool.

They did a test on Wyatt to see if he's able to

swallow. They gave him some disgusting milky liquid and then used a kind of x-ray machine to watch the white stuff go through his system. He did a good job swallowing, and it didn't go into his trache tube, but he couldn't do it fast enough. So they've scheduled him for another operation. They're going to put a feeding tube directly into his stomach so he won't have to be fed through the tube in his nose anymore.

Wyatt's operation is tomorrow, and I suddenly have a high fever, so I can't be near him until it goes away! I'm freaking out because I'm sick and I want to be with him for the surgery! I called the church. Ruthie's going to come and sit with him for the operation.

The last few months have been an emotional roller coaster. First they said he might not live, then they said he had no brain, then they said he had no corpus callosum and that he would never get off the ventilator and that he would die in the hospital! But guess what! He *has* a brain. He *has* a corpus callosum. He *is* off the ventilator. And he's coming home!! My little baby has defied them all. He has refused to give up and against all odds, we're going home!

I told the doctors in the last team meeting, "You never gave me any hope, you never encouraged me. All you did was tell me we could let him go. The nurses told me, the nurse practitioner told me. Everyone thought we should let him go and no one encouraged me." They were surprised and said they never meant to take my hope away. Apparently they've had a lot of parents accuse them of *not* warning them about the worst that might happen. So now they always make sure they tell people the worst. They apologized for not being more encouraging.

Wyatt has started having episodes and no one can figure out what's going on. We need to find out what this is before we can go home.

It's been a month since I last wrote. We're going back down to Boston. They found a growth called a granuloma formed in Wyatt's trache. He'll need to have it removed and they're going to put in a longer pediatric trache. That should take care of the problem.

This morning, Wyatt's nurse, Mary, looked at me with tears in her eyes. She sees that no matter what happens, I am *not* going to give up. She said that if *anyone* is going to get Wyatt home, it will be me. She told me I am a one of a kind mom and she believes I can make it happen. I *can* make it happen if it's God's will. I can do all things through Christ who strengthens me!

I was a little worried going down to Boston because of what happened last time, but everything went well and we were only there a couple of days. It was nice to see all the familiar faces but I'm glad to be on the way home.

It's Labor Day so a friend and I took Orianna to the fair. But the hospital called and we had to leave. When I got back here he was on the ventilator. I'm spending the night in the hospital because he is so sick. No one can figure out what happened …

I know what happened. One of the nurses down in Boston had a bad cold and *never* should have been around the babies. Wyatt ended up being on the ventilator for a week and a half and now that he's off, he has a blood infection. —Will it never end?

It's September 21st. Two more weeks have passed. The blood infection is gone and the doctors are talking about sending Wyatt home again. They've started training me on his home care and if all goes well, he will come home on September 30th.

During the team meeting, the doctor who's been so negative looked at me and said, "You know, you don't have to bring him home, there are other places he can go." I wanted to just yell at him, "GIVE ME A BREAK! When are you going to say hats off to you?" Why can't they just give credit where credit is due? I want my baby *home* with me. Is that so hard to understand?

Against all odds, my boy is coming home!

Wyatt is home! Thank God Wyatt is finally home! It is September 30th 2004. Wyatt is six months old today. My dad is here with the video camera and he got it all on tape. Now he's waiting for Orianna to get home from school so he can catch her reaction on film. It is so wonderful to finally have him home!

It's been over six months since Wyatt came home from the hospital. He's getting stronger all the time and he does something new every day. He's learned to give kisses and sometimes he smiles. He likes holding on to the bars of his crib and he's learning how to sit and hold his head up.

It's been a challenge becoming a single mom, because Brian is gone for good, but there are many people helping us. From Shelly at the fire station who helped me install Wyatt's special car seat, to the ladies at the church who continue to bring meals every week. One lady who's a friend of a friend gave me $500.00 just when I needed it, and I've found envelopes with money several times. People don't want credit, they just want to bless us. Orianna got to go to horse camp for free, and friends bring her to and from school every day. The Lord knows what we need and has continued to provide.

My dad has been a huge help. He's learned Wyatt's care so I can get out of the house or take a nap. He's helped us financially and emotionally and he's been good to talk to about Wyatt because twenty-two years ago he spent time in the NICU with my little brother . —And he always makes me think about the hard questions like, "Are you keeping Wyatt alive for Wyatt, or are you doing it for yourself?"

Orianna adores her little brother. Sometimes it's hard because she's no longer the center of attention. I know she wants to go out and hang out with Mommy the way we used to, but she understands that right now, Wyatt has to come first. She's been so brave, and I think God is preparing her for something.

Wyatt has a nurse who comes in for 28 hours each week. Marie is absolutely wonderful and sometimes I think she loves Wyatt more than I do! I don't know what I would do without her.

And finally I am thankful to God. Without him, I wouldn't have made it. James 4:8 says if you draw near to God that he will draw near to you. Daily I have sought him and he has never left us. Many people say they can feel the Lord's presence here and I think he and Wyatt have something worked out between them. My dad thinks Wyatt is not here for himself but that he's here for us— to teach us something— to show us something. I don't fully understand what Wyatt's purpose is yet, but God knows the end from the beginning, and I trust him.

I know I may not have Wyatt forever. I've told him many times if he wants to go home and be with his Father, it's alright. I know it would hurt, and it's the hardest thing to say, but I know I'd be alright. —But God hasn't taken him yet, and until he does, I will continue to love Wyatt every day. This is my journey and it is what the Lord has given me. I can either say 'No thank you,' or I can embrace it. And I am embracing it.

Wyatt has a shunt, a feeding tube and a trache and we're not sure if he can see or hear. His seizures have developed into infantile spasms. He needs twenty-four hour care but he's worth it. I look at him and I see the most beautiful little boy in the whole world. He has the most amazing brilliant blue eyes and the most perfect little lips. He's *so* cute. The Lord has blessed him with this awesome cuteness. He's always cuddly and I *never* think anything negative about him. I never think *why am I doing this?* Sometimes people say to me, "Oh it must be so hard…" but is it hard to love somebody? Is it hard to care for someone you love? No. I love him. He's my little boy— and he's perfect.

Wyatt is the strongest little person I have ever known. The doctors had to open his head up fifteen times in a three month period and he's had five different internalized shunts. He's endured thirty-three surgeries, several bouts of infection, numerous seizures and a host of other complications. They said he might not make it a week, but he's still here and he is over a year old.

No matter how many prayers were said, or how much *I* wanted him to live, he would have died if *he* had given up the fight. But he hasn't given up. He is a tough little guy, and has bravely faced each and every battle. He has fought for his life over and over again, and tasted sweet victory each and every time! He's my little trooper, my courageous little soldier.

Before he was born, God gave this little boy his name. And by the way, the name Wyatt— it means Little Warrior.

"Before I formed you in the womb,
I knew you…"
(Jeremiah 1:5 GW)

Jesus said,

"When I was hungry, you gave me something to eat, and when I was thirsty, you gave me something to drink... When I was sick, you took care of me..." Then the ones who pleased the Lord will ask, "When did we give you something to eat or drink?...or visit you while you were sick...?" The king will answer, "Whenever you did it for any of my people, no matter how unimportant they seemed, you did it for me."

(Mat 25:35-37,39-40 CEV)

Wyatt with big sister Orianna.

Jolted

Dave's Story

I've been a long-haul truck driver for thirty-four years, and only once do I remember falling asleep at the wheel. Well, I don't actually remember falling asleep, but I will never forget waking up.

It was back in the late 1980's, and I was doing a route I had done many times before. Starting from Maine, I had traveled down along the eastern seaboard to New Jersey where I had stopped to unload and pick up another trailer. From there I was driving through the night to reach my next stop outside of Boston at 8:00 AM. It was a hard trip, but I was used to doing it, and normally I had no trouble staying awake.

However, on this night, I was *tired.* I just could not keep my eyes open— and I nodded off. But before the truck went off the road, something jolted me awake. I was holding the wheel when something, or some*one,* touched me on the back of my left hand. And it was no ordinary touch. It felt as though someone's finger went right inside the back of my hand. Suddenly I was WIDE awake, and I remember saying, "Lord. You've got my attention!"

My hand went completely numb for six or eight hours! And I had no trouble staying awake for the rest of the trip.

I guess there are all kinds of ways for God, or one of his angels, to get your attention.

"Therefore let us not sleep, as do others; but let us watch and be sober."

(1Thesalonians 5:6 KJV)

Katahdin

Jamie's Story

Earlier in the day I had slipped and fallen.
And now I was petrified that I would slip again,
because now, there was nothing there to catch me.

We had never climbed Mount Katahdin before, so we didn't realize just how *long* it was going to take us to reach the top. At 5,267 feet, we reached the summit. We had been hiking for over eight hours, and it was four o'clock in the afternoon. That meant we had barely four and a half hours to make it back down to the base of the mountain before darkness overtook us. So with legs still shaking from the climb, my husband, my eighteen year old son, my sixteen year old daughter, and I, began the long descent.

After a couple of hours of scrambling backwards down over rocks and ladders, we reached the plateau near Thoreau Springs and paused to take a look around. From here we could see the trail above and below, and we took note that there was no one in sight in either direction for quite a long way. We filled our water bottles and moved on.

About an hour later we reached the area called Gateway (I call it *the gateway to HELL*) where the narrow pathway begins precariously winding its way along the top of sheer cliff areas. I for one, was *terrified!* Trying not to look down, I was gripped with fear. Earlier in the day I had slipped and fallen backwards against some rocks, and now I was *petrified* that I would slip again, because now, there was nothing there to catch me.

With my son taking the lead, and my husband bringing up the rear, we began scooting and crawling along the dangerous pathway. We were shaking with exhaustion and gripped with panic, and as we inched our way along, at first we were dead silent, but then my voice broke through the quiet. "Oh GOD. *Please* get us off this mountain! *Please* get us off this mountain!... " Over and over again, I pleaded for help.

And the light began to dim.

Suddenly, out of nowhere, another hiker appeared behind us. We didn't see him coming. We didn't *hear* him coming. He was just there. And without saying a word he began to help us. We made room for him to get by, but instead of moving on, he stayed with us for over an hour, helping us get over the rough spots, one step at a time.

As the path got a little easier, we had the opportunity to talk and get a better look at the man. His name was Steve, and he appeared to be in his late fifties. He was of medium build and his clothing looked like that of any other hiker. But his eyes were *so* blue, a pristine blue, and very deep. He talked about family, and he told us that he hiked the mountain every weekend. He also told us that he was a teacher.

At one point on the trail, we encountered another hiker. He was sitting on the ground in distress. Steve asked him if he was okay and the man told him he had run out of water. We were almost out of water ourselves, but Steve pulled out a brand new sealed bottle of water and gave it to the man.

When we reached the tree line, we parted company, and he was gone, just like that. We didn't see him again for the rest of the hike. And as we carefully picked our way through the darkness at the end of the trail, my husband spoke words that I will never forget.

He said, "You know God sent that angel to help us."

And I said, "I know."

We are deeply convinced that God heard our prayers and sent us a helper. If that kind teacher hadn't shown up, we would have had to spend the night on the mountain, completely unprepared. There's no doubt in my mind, that that man was an angel— if not the Lord himself.

"...the LORD will certainly have pity on you when you cry for help. As soon as he hears you, he will answer you."
(Isaiah 30:19 GW)

"The LORD may give you troubles and hardships. But your teacher will no longer be hidden from you. You will see your teacher with your own eyes."
(Isaiah 30:19-20 GW)

At the top of Katahdin.

Our Daily Bread

Laura's Story

Now it isn't unheard of for us to be invited out to dinner, but three times in one week?

My husband's job provides enough income for me to stay home with our two children, but there are times when we run out of money and have to call on God to provide. So far, he has never let us down.

One October I managed to get the bills paid on time, but there was nothing left to buy groceries, and we wouldn't get another paycheck for two weeks. I could have held back on the tithe, the ten percent we give back to God, and used that money for groceries, but I didn't do that. And I didn't waste a single moment worrying about it; God is always faithful to provide, and I think he really enjoys finding cool ways to give us what we need.

Now it isn't unheard of for us to be invited out to dinner, but three times in one week? On Monday night we had roast chicken, carrots, green beans, and mashed potatoes with gravy at my parents house. On Tuesday night we had spaghetti and the worlds *best* meatballs at a friends house. On Wednesday, eight bags of groceries miraculously appeared on my front steps. And on Thursday my cousin Kathy invited us out to Pat's Pizza for some *seriously* greasy pizza. (But if you mop up the grease with a pile of napkins, it's *awesome*. Really.)

So just as I knew he would, God provided enough food to get us through until the next paycheck, but he didn't do it the way I thought he did. *I* thought my friend, the one who made the best meatballs in the world on Tuesday night, was the one who brought us the groceries, because she was the *only* person I told about our food situation. But when I thanked her for the groceries, she told me *she* didn't buy them.

So my next thought was that she must have called the church and someone from there had deposited eight bags of groceries, hit the doorbell, and sprinted to their car (a light green four door) so they could speed off without being identified. But my friend told me she hadn't called the church either. She told me she had been home minding her own business when some friends showed up with groceries. They thought she could use them. But she didn't need groceries. So she told them our address, and they brought the groceries to our house, and stealth fully deposited them on our front steps. They didn't want to know who we were, and they didn't want us to know who they were. They knew if they did a good deed in secret, God would reward them openly.

"But when you do merciful deeds, do not let your left hand know what your right hand does, so that your merciful deeds may be in secret. And your Father who sees in secret Himself shall reward you openly."

(Matthew 6: 3-4 MKJV)

"So do not worry, saying, 'What shall we eat?' or 'What shall we drink?' ...But seek first his kingdom and his righteousness, and all these things will be given to you as well."

(Matthew 6:31-33 NIV)

Isn't God cool?

The Cross

Larry's Story

I started to cross before I saw it,
a little black car tearing around the curve
to make it through the light. I had just enough time
to form one thought. *She's got me.*

I think I've had a protector all my life. When I was three years old, I was run over by a big black car and there were tire marks all down my sleeve, but I was unharmed. When I was a little older, I was hit two winters in a row, on the same street, by the same man, in the same car. The first time I ended up unconscious in a snow bank, but both times I walked away with only a few minor scratches.

In the Navy I found myself in plenty of dangerous situations, but I was never seriously hurt. And one time, when I was stressed out and worrying, some unseen person spoke words of comfort to me. I had just put in for retirement, I was in Hawaii, and there was no way for me to go on job interviews in the states. I was walking around in my flight suit starting to panic, thinking, *What am I going to do? How am I going to support my family?* Then, clear as a bell, I heard a voice say, "God's going to take care of you. Don't worry."

But of all the times I've been protected, the following incident is the most amazing.

It was the winter of 1991, and I was at a safety conference in Brunswick, Maine. I had come down with a nasty cold and my head was throbbing, so when the instructor called for a break, I took the opportunity to run down the block to the drugstore. I needed some Tylenol.

I walked down to the crosswalk and paused. It was a busy two lane, one-way street, which curved out of sight. In the near lane, the traffic was stopped for the light, but the far lane was clear. I crossed between two vehicles in the first lane and slowed to look up the road. Nothing was coming.

What happened next is permanently etched in my memory.

I continued my stride out into the second lane when all of a sudden a little black car came *flying* around the curve at a breakneck speed. At a distance of about twenty-five feet, impact was imminent. There was no time to react. There was nowhere to go. I had just enough time to form one thought. *She's got me.*

In reflex, I began to step back— but then something unexplainable happened. I found myself surrounded by a cocoon of warm peace and protection, and instantly, I was back beside the car in the first lane and the little black car bumped the side of my knee. I was not afraid. I was not shaken up. In fact, I don't even think my heart rate went up.

The woman in the car was frantic.

I walked around the car and she rolled down the window. I calmly asked her, "Are you okay?" But she was a wreck. She was beside herself crying. And I gently told her, "It's alright. I'm okay. You didn't hit me."

In the Navy, I'd been in a lot of situations where I'd had the shakes, and when I walked into the drugstore I remember thinking, *The shakes are going to hit me any minute.* But they never did.

I've been around machinery all my life, and I've seen enough to know, if something is moving as fast as that little car was moving, there's no way it can stop in twenty-five feet. And I know how fast *I* can move.

There was no possible way for me to get out of the way of that car.

It wasn't luck, because there's no such thing as luck.

I think I've had a protector all my life.

And the peace and protection I experienced; something like that can only come from God.

***Jesus said, "Peace I leave with you,
My peace I give to you ... Let not your heart
be troubled, neither let it be afraid."***
(John 14:27 MKJV)

***"For surely, O LORD, you bless
the righteous; you surround them with
your favor as with a shield."***
(Psalm 5:12 NIV)

Erika's Angels

Erika's Story

We would *fly* through the air to get a hand under her head.
"Don't let her fall!" was like a mantra.

Viola Williams didn't like me very much, or at least I didn't think so. She was the only African American woman in our office, and she was a loner. For days she wouldn't even acknowledge me, but then, strangely enough, she would leave a little gift on my desk, and there would always be a Bible verse attached. In fact, when she did talk to me, she was always quoting scripture.

And like this wasn't weird enough, when I was nearing my due date with Erika, she asked if she could come to the hospital when I went into labor. I tried to discourage her; I barely knew the woman. But she was insistent, and ultimately I agreed to let her come.

I was in labor for fifteen hours, and Viola stayed at the hospital the entire time—praying. She sat out in the waiting room, and when my husband needed a break, she'd come into the delivery room. She would lay her hands on my leg and pray under her breath, and I remember thinking, *What's the big deal? People have babies every day!* My pregnancy had been perfectly normal. I just couldn't understand what all the praying was about.

When Erika was delivered, Viola was *thrilled.* Anyone would have thought it was her baby she was *so* excited. And this was very unlike her, because she was usually so reserved.

Four months later we found out, babies like Erika, usually die during childbirth or shortly thereafter.

"...pray one for another, that ye may be healed. The effectual fervent prayer of a righteous man availeth much"
(James 5:16 KJV)

First her belly button didn't heal, then her forearm swelled up for no apparent reason. She got bruises just from sitting in her car seat, and broken blood vessels in her mouth just from sucking. And sometimes there was blood in her stool. The doctors in North Carolina were at a loss, but when we moved home to Maine, her new doctor was determined to find out what was wrong. Two months later, Erika was diagnosed with an extremely rare form of hemophilia called Factor VII Deficiency.

> *Hemophilia is a hereditary blood disorder, in which a person has a deficiency or absence of certain clotting factors in their blood. In order to contract the disease, both parents have to be carriers. Symptoms of hemophilia can include; excessive bleeding, excessive bruising, nose bleeds, or abnormal menstrual bleeding. A person with hemophilia runs the risk of developing joint disease, vision loss, anemia, or neurological problems. Major blood loss or bleeding in a critical area, such as the brain, can be fatal.*
>
> *In the United States, there are approximately 18,000 people with hemophilia. The large majority have Factor VIII, or Factor IX Deficiency. Factor VII*

Deficiency is almost unheard of. There are only between twenty to thirty people alive in the United States today, who have Factor VII Deficiency.

Very little information was available, and what the doctor did find was all bad. We didn't know what to think. We had no idea we were carriers. All we knew was our baby girl had a deadly condition, and there was no treatment available in the U.S.

My supervisor's wife was a nurse, and as soon as she heard of Erika's diagnosis, she went into the hospital library to photocopy everything she could find on Factor VII Deficiency. What she found was very bleak. In every case study, the child had ended up dying. She found nothing that offered even a glimmer of hope, and she didn't want to give me the photocopies. She thought I was better off not knowing.

Two weeks later her husband put an envelope on my desk. He indicated there was nothing hopeful inside, but he wanted me to have it anyway, because he thought I had a right to know.

I didn't want to open it. I didn't think I could take any more bad news, and I let it sit there. *I won't read it. Not now. Not here. I'll wait until the weekend, when I have time to cry.*

But something kept nagging at my heart. I *needed* to read it. I didn't want to, but I felt compelled, so I picked up the envelope. There were pages of medical jargon, most of which I didn't understand, but one case study stood out to me. It was about an infant who had died of a brain hemorrhage, and one of the symptoms he'd displayed, was a bulging soft spot.

That night, Erika had a brain hemorrhage.

It was May 8, 1990, and in the middle of the night, Erika started crying and vomiting. I immediately called the doctor and described what was going on. When I asked about a brain hemorrhage, he said if she wasn't having seizures, then a brain hemorrhage was unlikely. He told me to give her Pedialite and to call him back in two hours. But after hanging up the phone, I remembered the case study and put my hand on my baby's head. Immediately I called back. Erika's soft spot was bulging.

At the ER they diagnosed a brain hemorrhage and started giving her fresh frozen plasma to build up the clotting factor in her blood. We had to wait four long hours until it was safe to operate, and the doctors told us she *wasn't* going to make it. But she *did* make it. They were able to operate in time, and she pulled through.

If I had waited two hours and then called back, Erika would have died. But because I had read *that* case study *that* day, she survived. It was a miracle. There's no doubt in my mind.

As time went on, treatment was found for Erika. Because of spontaneous bleeds, usually deep in a muscle, she needs to have a shot of Factor VII concentrate every other day. Growing up, Erika rarely had spontaneous bleeds, but the threat of an accident and subsequent blood loss was always a constant concern.

The day Erika took her first step was both exciting, and terrifying, all at the same time. For the next year, "*Don't let her fall!*" was like a mantra. And if she stumbled, we would *fly* through the air to get a hand under her head before she hit the ground.

Miraculously, she learned to walk without any major accidents, but there was no time to relax— because then she started *running*. She would fly around the house and time after time we'd see her veer straight towards a door casing— but she never hit one. Never! And we were forever in awe and amazement, looking at each other saying, “How did *that* happen?” We were sure she was going to smash right into a sharp corner, but somehow she would cruise right by, just missing it.

She must have had more than one guardian angel.

She doesn't remember these early days, but she does remember one near accident when she was five.

I was playing bat and ball with my dad. I was only five and he was trying to throw it so I could hit it, but this one time he threw it too far, then he turned to go back towards our garage.

The ball went over my head, and when I reached up with the bat, my foot slipped, and I started to fall backwards. I thought I was going to land on my head on the pavement— and it scared me! I can remember thinking, If I hit the ground, this is going to be bad!

But then, all of a sudden I stopped falling. I felt a hand on my back steadying me. It was a large hand, like a big man's hand, and there was a tingling feeling, like something was giving me strength. I was tipping way back, but it held me there until I got my balance, and then I stood up.

I looked around, but there was no one there. And I ran into the garage yelling, “Mom! Dad! An angel helped me!”

I had never fallen that hard before, so thinking about hitting my head on the pavement, and then feeling myself being pushed back up... it was God! I don't know how else to say it!

"For he will command his angels concerning you to guard you in all your ways; they will lift you up in their hands..."
(Psalm 91: 11-12 NIV)

"Behold, I send an Angel before you, to keep you in the way, and to bring you to the place which I have prepared."
(Exodus 23:20 MKJV)

****

At five months of age, when she had her brain hemorrhage, Erika's right frontal lobe was disabled. At two and a half, she lost the vision in her right eye. Today, at fifteen, she has a spontaneous bleed somewhere in her body approximately once every ten to fourteen days. She can't play sports. She can't jump rope. She can't roller blade. She's tried these things and they all cause bleeding. And yet, she is the most optimistic person I know.

She is always an encouragement, I think because she herself has been through so much. And when someone is having problems, she really *listens,* and never fails to direct them to prayer, often praying with them right on the spot.

Each and every day, Erika continues to be a bright spot in our lives. Her wit is quick and her laughter abundant, and her love for young and old is evident in the flash of her brilliant smile. Not only is she a miracle, she is truly a blessing from above.

Some of Erika's favorite verses:

"For I know the thoughts
that I think toward you, saith the LORD,
thoughts of peace, and not of evil,
to give you an expected end."
(Jeremiah 29:11 KJV)

"always giving thanks
for all things to God the Father in the
name of our Lord Jesus Christ,"
(Ephesians 5:20 MKJV)

"Trust in the LORD with all
your heart, and do not lean on your own
understanding. In all your ways acknowledge
him, and he will make straight your paths."
(Proverbs 3:5-6 ESV)

Pierced

Nancy's Story

I wanted to get up and take the bread, but I wasn't allowed. I slouched down and peeked up at the people waiting in line. In the whole church, only three others were still sitting. To me, not being able to take the bread, meant that I wasn't good enough.

They told me God loved me— but I wasn't convinced.

I tried smoking pot when I was twelve.
By fourteen, I was getting high every day.
I dressed to get the boys attention.
At fifteen, my baby sitter's boyfriend abused me.
I tried cocaine... and acid...
and started binging and purging.
But Nothing filled the emptiness.

When I was still in high school I moved in with my boyfriend. Rob was good to me at first. But it wasn't long before he started abusing me. I put up with it for several months, but the night he ripped the phone out of the wall and sent me to the hospital with a ruptured eardrum, I'd had enough. The next day I moved back home.

But then I met another man. Gary was fun loving and we both loved to party, so it made perfect sense to move in with him. But then *he* started abusing me. At first it was only with words, but after I got pregnant and decided to keep the baby, the abuse began to get worse.

I had quit smoking and drinking, but I would still go out with Gary to the bars, and one night when we got home after he had been drinking heavily, I said something that made him mad and he shoved me hard. I shoved him back and the next thing I knew I was on the floor with him on top of my pregnant belly. This sent me into labor.

So again I moved home. And even though we tried to reconcile for the sake of our child, we never did get back together.

After having my daughter, Brooke, I became overwhelmed with the responsibility of being a single mom, and with life in general, so I started smoking pot again. And my binging and purging got so bad, the purging became easy. I barely had to try at all to make it happen.

I knew I had a problem.

I sought professional help. I was diagnosed with Attention Deficit Disorder and depression, and my doctor put me on depression medication so I would stop binging and purging. He also suggested I see a therapist.

I thought the therapist would tell me to stop smoking pot. But he didn't. He told me, in my case, smoking pot was actually *good* for me! He said it had a calming effect on my ADD, and he saw no reason for me to stop.

In three years, I saw a psychiatrist, a nutritionist, a Master of Social Work, a psychologist, and a Licensed Clinical Social Worker. I was put on Paxil, Prozac, Welbutrin, Zoloft, Buspar, and a mood stabilizer. But all of these drugs only masked my feelings, and caused side effects. The pull to the refrigerator, and the need to get into an altered state were still there— so I continued to drink, and binge, and smoke pot...

At the age of twenty-one, I completed beauty school and managed to get a job and a place of my own. However, I still craved attention and a sense of belonging, so I was always looking for a "good" man. Then I met Matt. At first he was fun, but early on he became very controlling and suspicious. I never moved in with him, but the whole time we were seeing each other he was sure I was cheating on him. So after awhile, I told him I didn't want to see him anymore. —But he wouldn't leave me alone.

Then one day while I was cutting a woman's hair, I began telling her about this ex-boyfriend who was harassing me. I felt I could open up to her because she was somehow different from most of my other customers. She would always ask how I was doing, and how my daughter was, and she was always very interested in what I had to say. So I started telling her about Matt, and I thought maybe she would sympathize, but instead— she started quoting things from the Bible! I stood there trying to maintain my composure, but I couldn't believe what she was saying. She told me what *God* had to say about me, and even suggested that I had brought my problems on myself by the way I was living. How dare she say I was "living in sin"! What a whack job! This time when I finished her hair, I was glad to see her leave.

But then she came back a few weeks later and did it again! What a Froot Loop! Time and time again she came back. And it got to the point that whenever I saw the name Ann in the appointment book, I *dreaded* her coming. Didn't she know it wasn't okay to talk about religion in public? Clearly this woman was just a little bit *off,* but what could I say? We were taught in beauty school, to *never* talk about religion or politics with clients.

So I was polite to her, but I wasn't going to change the way I was living for her sake. If I wanted to live in sin and binge and smoke pot (hey, the "professional" told me it was alright) then that's what I was going to do! Nothing she had to say about *God* was going to change anything. Besides, God probably didn't love me anyway; I was never allowed to take the bread.

Then one day I dropped Brooke off at the sitter and decided to go out for a walk before getting ready for work. When I got back, I went into the bathroom and turned on my curling iron— then nearly had a heart attack when Matt stepped out from behind the shower curtain!

I *screamed* at him to get out, but he *demanded* to know *where* I had been and *who* I was seeing. We started shoving each other and the next thing I know I was on the floor and he had his hands around my throat. I couldn't breathe! I flailed my arms and legs, and I guess he realized what he was doing, because he loosened his grip, and I somehow managed to get up and grab my hot curling iron. When he came screaming at me again, I warned him, but he kept coming, so I hit him on the face with the red hot iron. He smashed his fist against my ear and I kept screaming at him to get out and get out of my life! Finally he took the hint and stormed out.

I probably would have called in sick, but I was the new assistant manager, and I *had* to go to work. When I got there, my ear was still swollen and I was still shaking, and who should be there but Bob, the nut case's husband. He saw how upset I was and started asking questions. I ended up crying and telling him everything.

The next day Ann showed up. This time she didn't just tell me what God had to say about me, she actually took her Bible out of her bag and started pointing out scriptures! In my head, I was thinking, "Oh *great,* here we go again!"

But in my spirit, the words just *pierced* through me.

"Know ye not that the unrighteous shall not inherit the kingdom of God? Be not deceived: neither fornicators, nor idolaters, nor adulterers, nor effeminate, nor abusers of themselves with mankind, nor thieves, nor covetous, nor drunkards, nor revilers, nor extortioners, shall inherit the kingdom of God."
(1 Corinthians 6:9-10 KJV)

I knew what she was showing me was the truth. But then I met Brian. He was perfect! He had his own business, he loved my daughter, he loved to party. —And he loved me. Who could be more perfect? So after taking it slow at first, we rented an apartment together. I wanted to buy a house so I could start my own salon, so I thought maybe we could save up and buy a house together.

And then Ann started inviting me to church. After awhile, even though I still thought she was different, I decided to go. I went with her a few times and then one Easter Sunday, when the pastor asked if anyone wanted to accept Jesus as their Savior and have their sins forgiven— I raised my hand.

Finally, I got to take the bread, *The* Bread, The Bread of Life. Jesus.

"And Jesus said to them, I am the bread of life. He who comes to Me shall never hunger, and he who believes on Me shall never thirst."
(John 6:35 MKJV)

At this point, Ann bought me my very own Bible. And wasn't she excited! Then she invited me to a women's retreat in Cape Cod. My spirit had come alive and I now felt a hunger for something else. Something more. So I went to the retreat, and roomed with the "nut case" and three of her friends. This was a real turning point in my life. I was baptized and truly began to see the world through new eyes, and it was there in that room in Cape Cod that I learned what God's will is for His children. I also learned the importance of daily Bible reading and that the Gospel of John was a good place to start.

Back at home, Brian said I changed right before his eyes. We would still go out, but it wasn't the same. I would still occasionally smoke pot, but now there was a sense of unrest about it. And even though I loved Brian and he was good to me, I decided to trust what the Bible said about the way I was living, and I moved back in with my parents. I continued to see Brian, but something in my heart told me he wasn't the one for me.

Soon after this, Brian went to a school reunion and met an old girlfriend. Three months later they were married.

I continued to trust God and put into practice what I was reading in my Bible— and God started working miracles. A client of mine was selling a house that I desperately wanted to buy. It was the perfect size, in a nice area, and it even had room for a salon. But there was no way I could afford it— so I started going to the house and praying. I would park in the driveway and pray. Then I got the keys and went inside and prayed some more. For over a month I prayed. And whenever I started feeling overwhelmed, I would recite this scripture, and it brought me peace.

***"Be anxious about nothing,
but in everything by prayer and by
petition with thanksgivings, let your requests
be made know to God; and the peace of God
which surpasses all understanding will
keep your hearts and your minds
in Christ Jesus."***
(Philippians 4:6-7 LITV)

On paper, there was no way I could afford to buy the house.

But I bought it anyway. I took a step of faith.

I had exactly $517.00 in my savings account. The owners wanted only $500.00 down! And they were asking $711.00 a month to owner finance the house. This was far more than I could afford. But somehow, someway, every month, I managed to pay the bills. Even the curtains I had bought for my apartment matched *perfectly* with the curtains already in the house. I knew God was answering my prayers!

First, against all odds, and without the help of a man, I bought a house and started my own salon. Then I started praying for a husband. "Lord, can you bring me someone who really loves me, loves Brooke as his own, and of course, loves You with all his heart! —And, oh yeah, it would be great if he could cook too."

—Then I met Mike at church.

I will never forget the night I was looking in the mirror and praying about Mike. I felt the Lord say to my heart, "He is going to be your husband." And he was! He is! After so many failed attempts at relationships, I finally trusted God to show me who I should marry, and I am now married to a man who is good to me, who completes me. —And, oh yeah, he used to be the head chef in a restaurant!

God was working in my life and the more I trusted him, the more he healed me. I didn't have to clean up my act. I came as I was and slowly he came in and began to clean my house, one room at a time.

After smoking pot almost every day for fourteen years, I was able to stop. After struggling with an eating disorder for more than ten years, I met Sandy and Kelly, two women who had struggled with the same problem. Whenever I was tempted to binge, I would call one of them and they would pray with me, helping me get through, without the use of drugs.

I had finally come to a place where I *knew* that God loved me, and I didn't need drugs, or alcohol, or food, or therapy, or anything else to fill the void. All I needed, was Jesus.

Mike and Nancy have been married for eight years and have added two children to their family. Their marriage has had many ups and downs, but God has been faithful to get them through the rough times.

There have been times when Nancy was tempted and fell back into old sinful habits, but she was quick to repent and turn back to the Lord for forgiveness and comfort. He has never let her down.

"... God is faithful,
and he will not let you be tempted
beyond your ability, but with the temptation
he will also provide the way of escape,
that you may be able to endure it."
(1 Corinthians 10:15 ESV)

I don't know where I'd be if Ann hadn't been so persistent. For close to two years she and her family prayed for me, but I resisted everything she had to say. I didn't want to listen, but when she took her Bible out of her bag, and actually pointed out the words, they *pierced* through all my defenses.

"For the Word of God is
living and powerful and sharper
than any two-edged sword, piercing even to the
dividing apart of soul and spirit..."
(Hebrews 4:12 MKJV)

Now when I'm doing someone's hair, and they tell me their problems, I'm the one likely to pull my Bible out of my bag, to tell them what *God* has to say about things.

Amy Carmichael of India once asked a stonecutter which blow of the hammer broke the stone. He answered, "The first, and the last— and every one in between."

When you are speaking the truth in love (Eph. 4:15) don't become frustrated if you think nothing is happening. As the Spirit leads, just keep on hammering, because, even though you may not see it, just below the surface, the door to someone's heart may be opening.

"so shall My Word be,
which goes out of My mouth;
it shall not return to Me void,
but it shall accomplish that
which I please..."
(Isaiah 55:11 LITV)

Make It Blue

Stephanie's Story

One winter, when we were just barely getting by, our car died. So I prayed this prayer. "Dear Lord, we need a car, and we only have four hundred dollars. Could you make it a station wagon, because we have four kids. And oh—could you make it blue?"

Three days later, a Volvo station wagon appeared with a sign on it two houses down. It was for sale. It was $400.00. And it was blue.

"And all things,
whatever you shall ask in prayer,
believing, you shall receive."
(Matthew 21:22 MKJV)

Take My Hand

Sandy's Story

We wanted to have a baby right away. It didn't matter that we already had three beautiful girls from my first marriage to care for, we wanted a baby of our own, so I got pregnant right away.

At first the pregnancy was going along very well, but then something went very wrong. At the end of my first trimester I started spotting and ended up having a miscarriage. Nothing like this had ever happened to me before. I had always become pregnant quickly, had easy pregnancies, and bore healthy babies. The loss of this baby was devastating, and for weeks I grieved.

But after some time had passed we were ready to try again. This time I went to the doctor for a check up. He examined me, did a pap smear, and gave us the go ahead to try for another baby.

Five weeks later I received a notice in the mail. It was my test results, and they weren't good. The pap had revealed "displaced cells." I needed to call my doctor right away.

On the phone, the nurse gave me information beyond what my mind was able to comprehend. There would have to be tests taken, because this could be an indication of cervical cancer. She kept talking, "... cells... tests... biopsy... surgery... invasive... hysterectomy..."

But my mind had frozen up at the word cancer.

I went in and they took tissue samples from my cervix for further testing. Results revealed that I had carcinoma in situ III, stage three of cervical cancer. Two thirds to the full thickness of my cervix was cancerous. And to make matters worse, it was likely the cancer would soon reach my uterus, if it wasn't there already.

They also discovered, that I was pregnant.

The doctor wanted to do what's called a laser conization immediately. This would remove the cancerous part of my cervix and determine if the cancer had reached my uterus. It was imperative I do this right away to stop the cancer as soon as possible, BUT, it was likely to cause another miscarriage. The doctor laid out our options. I could go ahead with the procedure and risk having a miscarriage; I could have an abortion, do the procedure, and get pregnant again after the cancer was dealt with; or I could go on with the pregnancy and be closely monitored to see if the cancer was spreading. This latter option would put both the baby *and* me at risk.

Taking the life of our child was not an option and we were grieved the doctor would even suggest it. However, we understood the longer we waited, the more likely the cancer would become life threatening. If I had the test, I was risking the life of my baby, but if I didn't have the test, I was taking the chance of losing the baby *and* leaving my husband without a wife, and my three girls without a mother.

One of my neighbors was in nursing school so I borrowed her books and read everything I could about my situation. What I read matched what the doctor was telling us; his urgency was justified.

As much as we wanted this baby, we now began praying that God would take it away.

I began going in every few days for blood work. The hormone indicating pregnancy, or HCG, was increasing with each test. This indicated a viable pregnancy. Again the doctor asked us to consider an abortion. Again we made it clear that abortion was not an option. We continued to pray, our church family at Calvary Baptist was praying, and our friends at Penobscot Christian School were praying. We even had people at a friend's church in Florida praying for us. All we wanted was for God to either bless the pregnancy— or take the child.

And I was at peace. I had every reason to be stressed out and anxious, but as we continued to pray for God's guidance, there was peace.

Two weeks after my diagnosis, I woke up one morning and discovered that I was bleeding. When I miscarried the first time, it was devastating, but this time, there was a sense of elation. God had made his decision— and I knew everything was going to be fine.

That day my husband came to the doctor's with me. The doctor presented us with a D+C, a procedure to dilate my cervix and remove the inner lining of my uterus. This would speed up my recovery so he could go ahead with the laser conization. My husband and I looked at each other. If there was any chance the baby was still alive and had a chance of surviving, we were not going to have anything to do with destroying it. The doctor was insistent and wanted to do the D+C on the spot, so we asked for some time to pray.

Our prayers were intense, and as we prayed, we both knew it was okay to go on with the procedure. There was a complete peace about the decision; somehow we both felt sure, that the baby was already gone.

The procedure was excruciatingly painful and I realized as it went on, that it was the same procedure used to preform abortions. It was absolutely horrible— and it gave me a small glimpse of what women go through physically and emotionally when they have an abortion.

When it was over, I was scheduled for the laser conization in two weeks, but a few days later, a nurse called and said I needed to come back in. I could tell by the tone of her voice that she was surprised at what she had to tell me; there wasn't a *trace* of chorionic (HCG) found in my amniotic fluid when it was tested in the lab. Only a few hours had passed between when I'd started bleeding and when I'd had the D+C. There *should* have been chorionic in the fluid. The nurse told me, maybe the doctor "hadn't gotten it all."

The record was clear. My HCG levels were increasing with each blood test, so there was no doubt that I had, in fact, been pregnant. When I went in for another blood test, the HCG level had dropped significantly, indicating that the doctor hadn't "missed anything." So why wasn't there any HCG in my fluid?

A short time later I was telling my story to a friend when suddenly I knew. There wasn't any chorionic in the fluid because God wanted to reassure us that the baby was gone before the D+C was performed. He wanted us to know beyond a shadow of a doubt that we did not have any part in taking our baby's life. Loud and clear he was saying to me, "You did not take your baby. I did. When you seek me and I take care of things, I am complete. I love you and I am going to take care of you." It still blows my mind every time I think about it.

The laser conization removed the cancer from my cervix, and the cancer had not reached my uterus. I was declared cancer free. A few months later I became pregnant with our daughter, Ashley.

"...And the LORD shall guide thee continually..."

(Isaiah 58:9,11 KJV)

While Ashley was still a baby, my husband was also diagnosed with cancer. For close to two years, our lives were completely unpredictable with hospital visits, tests, and treatments. And it wasn't long before I found myself getting thoroughly stressed out.

Then one day while walking through the hospital parking lot with my girls, Brittney, my five year old, refused to hold my hand. She was terrified that at any moment she was going to get hit by a car— but she would *not* hold my hand. I was frustrated with her stubbornness and I thought, *Why does she have to do everything herself! Why won't she just take my hand?* Then suddenly I realized something. I was doing the same thing with God! I was getting stressed out and scared and I felt the Lord speak to my heart. "*You're scared of things you can't control, but all you need to do is take MY hand, and I will guide you through.*

"For I the LORD thy God will hold thy right hand, saying unto thee, Fear not; I will help thee.

(Isaiah 41:13 KJV)

Soon after this my husband was declared cancer free.

That Still Small Voice

Jean's Story

It was another wonderful ordinary day at my beloved camp. And there I stood at my kitchen sink, washing dishes, and looking out the window at the trees gently moving in the wind.

My eyes kept returning to one tree in particular. It was right next to the driveway. My car was parked beside it.

That tree is going to fall.

What? That's dumb. Why would I think that? It doesn't look like it's going to fall. It's windy— but it's not *that* windy.

That tree is going to fall. You should move the car.

No. That's stupid.

Ten minutes passed and the thought kept bugging me.

—So I went out and backed my car up a few feet.

Twenty minutes later *that* tree fell in the driveway—right where my car had been!

I immediately thanked the Lord for saving my car.

My thoughts on this experience: That inner voice we sometimes hear, should be *listened* to, and taken *very* seriously!

"Be still, and know that I am God:..."

7 (Psalm 46:10 KJV)

The Nurse's Aide

Marie's Story

There are many miracles,
especially when a person puts all their faith in God.

The miracle that started my career as a nurse happened in 1971 when I realized I had to provide for my family. I had taught dance lessons before I was married and then was a housewife with six children for many years, so my experience in the work force was extremely limited. My neighbor, an Italian woman, was also looking for work. She had plenty of experience, but she couldn't write English, so we decided to combine forces and help each other out.

The morning we were to start our job hunt, I went to Mass and knelt at the altar. With total faith, I asked Jesus to help me find a job.

First we went to St. Joseph Hospital where I helped my neighbor fill out an application. Since she had spent many years working in a pizza parlor she was hired, on the spot, to work in the kitchen. I, however, did not get a job. They were not going to hire someone who had no experience. I was a little disheartened but we moved on to the next place on our list, Downey Community Hospital. This time before we went in, I prayed. "Please, God, I need a job."

Now as a rule, when you enter any large hospital, there is a desk with volunteers who answer questions and help people find their way around. But at this hospital, we were greeted right at the door. The man looked to be around forty years old, and he wanted to know if there was anything he could do to help us. I remember thinking how much he looked like my brother, Maurice, except for his eyes. Maurice's eyes were brown, this man's were very blue.

I told him, "I need a job. I have no experience. I've been a housewife for many years, but I'm willing to do anything, scrub floors, clean bathrooms, any menial job. Anything."

He lead us to the back of the hospital, towards the right, and down a hallway to his office. Once there, he told me that if I would go and take classes to become a nurse's aide, he would give me a job. Then he called in his secretary. She looked to be in her fifties, and seemed very bashful. He asked her to go and find out where and what time the nurse's aide class was going to be that night. She smiled sweetly at us, then went and did as he asked.

A few months later, after I was trained, the teacher took me aside and told me I should go and put in an application at a certain hospital. She told me not to tell anyone else about the opening. I did as she said, and I was hired! Just like that.

At this point, I went back to Downey Hospital to thank the man who had helped me. But when I asked about him at the desk, no one knew who I was talking about. I described him, telling them how tall he was, and that he had dark hair, side burns, and beautiful blue eyes, but they just looked at each other. They couldn't think of anyone who matched that description. I described the man's secretary. They didn't know who she was either. So I set out on my own to find his office— but I couldn't find it! I walked all over the place where I remembered it being. It just wasn't there.

They did have an employment office— but it was on a different floor.

I believe Jesus sent an angel to help me.

In 1977, I was working nights as an LVN (Licensed Vocational Nurse) and had started taking classes during the day to become an RN, but it was very difficult and I felt I was neglecting my home, so I decided to give it up. But before I quit, I went out to breakfast with another nurse, Mary Doolittle, and she told me *not* to give up. She knew about a special class where, if you had three or four years of LVN experience, you could go and become an RN in only one year.

I went home and told my son Wade about this class, and he said I should give it a try. —But I didn't go right away and the next night while I was at work, Wade called me three times telling me I shouldn't put it off any longer or the class would get filled up. He was very persistent.

I asked a co-worker to go with me and we went the very next day to the college where Mary said the class was going to be. A group of people were coming out of a room and we asked them where we needed to go to sign up. They were amazed and asked how we knew about the class. They had just found out about it themselves! But they told us where to go and we were the first ones to sign up.

The next day we were told that the class was only for LVNs at a different hospital, and they gave us our money back. But then they said to call back later, and if anyone dropped out, they would make an exception and let us in. When we called later, five people had dropped out.

During the time when I was taking this class, Mary Doolittle asked me where I had heard about it. I told her, "YOU told me!"

She didn't remember.

I told Wade, "It's a good thing you kept calling me about signing up for this class. I almost missed the opportunity."

He said, "I never called you."

When my mother was still alive, it was very difficult finding private time with her. So occasionally we would buy McDonald's food for the kids and then go park the car in front a little restaurant. We would go inside, sit by the front window, and have a quiet lunch together while watching the kids eat their lunch in the car. Well, one day, we were doing this and one of the kids released the emergency brake! The car started rolling backwards towards the road and I bolted out the door. But before I got to the car, I saw a man who looked like a truck driver get behind the car and stop it. I jumped in the car and pulled up the emergency brake, but when I turned around to look, the man was gone. In a few seconds, he had vanished.

Another time, there was a nurse at work who wanted to get even with me because I got the job she was trying to get. First she smashed my headlights. Then one day I was driving on the freeway when a man in a car to my right started beeping his horn at me. He motioned that I should get off the freeway. Immediately I had a feeling that something was wrong. I took the next exit and there was a tire store right there. I stopped to have the car checked and they found two large staples in both of my back tires. If I had kept driving, I might have been involved in a major accident, putting my life, and the lives of others in danger.

There was no way the man on the freeway could have known anything was wrong with my car.

—Unless perhaps he was an angel.

***"The angel of the
LORD encampeth round
about them that fear him,
and delivereth them."***
(Psalm 34:7 KJV)

***"For he shall give his
angels charge over thee, to keep
thee in all thy ways."***
(Psalm 91:11KJV)

A Simple Prayer

Autumn's Story

It was a frigid cold day deep in the heart of evergreen country where a little girl stood holding her mama's hand in the snow covered driveway. The mama looked down at the little girl and made a sad face. "Honey, our van won't start and we don't know why. Grampy doesn't know what's wrong with it, and Daddy doesn't either. Do you think we should ask God for help?"

The little girl looked up with big serious eyes and nodded.

So the mama prayed. "God, our van won't start and we don't have any money to get it fixed. You say in the Bible, if we need something, we should ask. Well, it sure would be nice to have our van working again. Please help us. In Jesus name we pray…" She looked down and smiled at her little daughter who finished the prayer.

"Am-en." (Which sounded more like, "I'm in.")

"Now won't it be fun to see how God fixes our van?"

A couple of days later, the little girl's uncle (who had never been particularly concerned about other people's vehicles before) suddenly decided to do something. He commissioned the services of his mechanic friend and together the two of them came and fixed the van right there in the driveway- in the rain. The uncle paid for the part, and the friend refused the offer to pay him later. He was just glad to help.

And the mama said as she strapped her little girl into her car seat, “Wasn’t it fun to see how God answered our prayer? I never called a tow truck. I never called a mechanic. I never asked Uncle Kenny for help. I didn’t make one phone call, and I didn’t spend a dime. All I did was say a simple prayer, and now our van is running perfectly. Isn't God amazing?” She looked into the eyes of her little daughter. “We should thank God for this blessing.”

The little girl nodded seriously.

So the mama prayed, “Dear Lord, thank you for giving us Uncle Kenny and his friend, Elliot, so our van could be fixed. It's really great to have our van running again. Thank you so much for all You do for us. In Jesus name we pray...”

The little girl snuggled down into her car seat, smiled, and said, “I'm in!”

Jesus said,
“… Truly, truly, I say to
you, whatever you shall ask
the Father in My name,
He will give you.”
(John 16:23 MKJV)

Take My Life

Jeremiah's Story

"If there's a God who loves me, then he can have me.
I don't want my life anymore.
I don't want control anymore.
If I have control,
I'm going to kill myself."

My whole life I was looking for love in the wrong places. Humans want to be loved and we want to be needed. I wanted that feeling my whole life, maybe because my parents are divorced, maybe because I'm just messed up. I don't know.

Every Sunday, from as far back as I can remember, we went to church.

When I was ten, I started breaking into buildings.

My father was a narcotics officer.

When I was fourteen, I started selling drugs.

I was a bad kid.

By the time I finished high school, my criminal record included: petty theft, possession of drugs, and shoplifting. And this was only what they caught me doing. I was the guy people looked at and said, "He'll never amount to anything." I was the guy who would die of liver cancer by the time I was twenty-six. I was the guy who would end up in prison long before that.

My mother got me a good job in a hospital, but I was drinking every night and hungover every day. Then after I wrecked my new jeep and got a DUI, not only did I lose my vehicle, I lost my license, my job, and my house.

So I went to live in a fraternity. I never went to a

single class at Fresno State, but I lived there for a year and a half— because I could drink a lot. In fact, it got so bad, I started carrying a tape recorder in my chest pocket so I could remember what I'd done the night before.

Then I started doing a lot of drugs.

And one night, I tried to kill myself.

But it didn't work.

I woke up the next morning, curled up in a fetal position on the floor, crying. Vomit was everywhere. And I remember praying, "If there's a God who loves me, then he can have me! I don't want my life anymore. I don't want control anymore. If I have control, I'm going to kill myself!"

Jesus said,

"For whosoever will save his life shall lose it: but whosoever will lose his life for my sake, the same shall save it"

(Luke 9:24 KJV)

That day there was a newsletter in the fraternity mailbox. It was from a Christian camp called Hume Lake, and it was addressed to me. This was weird, because no one had my address at the fraternity, and I had never gotten mail there before.

I'd gone to this camp as a sophomore in high school, so I was familiar with it. The newsletter said they were hiring, and something told me I should apply, so I did.

When I got to the camp I asked the ladies in the office, "How did I get here? Explain this to me please. How did I get this newsletter when no one has my address?"

They searched their files, but they couldn't find the address. I couldn't have gotten a newsletter from them.

They said it was impossible.

So I started thinking— maybe there is a God.

I quit drugs and alcohol (since they weren't available) and I started working as a cashier at the camp diner. I had a lot of time in between customers, so I started reading the Bible, and one day I read something that sounded wrong. Jesus said that he didn't come to bring peace, but a sword. *What? I thought Jesus wanted everybody to be friends! You know, peace on earth?* Then I read that he said love your enemies, and if someone hits you, you should let them hit you again. *WHAT? No! If someone hits you, you hit them back!*

I had gone to church my whole life, but this was the first time I'd read the Bible for myself. I didn't understand what Jesus was saying, but I wanted to know more, so I kept reading. And one day, I read that Jesus claimed to *be* God. He said in John 8, "...before Abraham was, I Am." So I started thinking, either Jesus was *completely* nuts— or he was actually God.

Then one day I had the day off and wanted to go fishing. I didn't have a pole, and I didn't have any money, so I went to the office and asked the ladies if I could get an advance on my pay. They told me they couldn't do that. —Then they asked if I had prayed about it.

Prayed about it? You people are crazy! So what will happen? I'll PRAY for a fishing pole and one will just SHOOT out of the wall? You and your Christian... WHATEVER! Did I PRAY about it? That's just so stupid! It's the dumbest thing I've ever heard.

So I prayed about it. I did it out of spite. But I did it. "God can I have a fishing pole, 'cause I really want to go fishing. It's nothing bad. I'm not doing drugs anymore. I'm not drinking. So can I at least have a fishing pole?"

When I got back to my trailer, my roommate came in and asked what was up. I told him— and he handed me thirty bucks to go buy a fishing pole.

All right God.

So I got into this prayer thing. The first thing I prayed about was what to do when the summer was over. I didn't want to go back to my hometown, that was not an option. I knew myself well enough to know what would happen if I went back into that situation.

Then the lady at the post office started telling me about this place called Joshua. She said, "You should go to this place. It's a discipleship program. You go there and study the Bible. You can't listen to music. You can't watch movies. You can't date. You separate yourself from the world— for nine months."

So I said, "You got any other ideas?"

People kept talking to me about this place, and I lied to them. I said, "I would *love* to go to Joshua, but I can't afford it. It costs $8,000.00 and *unfortunately* for me, I just don't have that kind of money."

Then my mother called and said, "I heard you want to go to Joshua. I'll pay for it if you want to go."

How did my mother find out about Joshua? I hadn't talked to her in weeks! "Mom, who told you about Joshua? And who told you I wanted to go there? I certainly don't want to go there! I can't listen to music. I can't date. Does that sound like something I would want to do? —And besides, I think it's filled up."

My mom insisted that I go and ask if there were any openings, so just to get her off my back, I told her I would. But I had no intention of doing so.

And then this thing started bugging me. And it wouldn't stop. So I went and talked to the director. "I know you have a waiting list of like a hundred people... but my mother's offered to pay for me... so I just want to let you know... because I keep feeling this *thing* telling me to do stuff... and I've got to tell you so it'll quit bugging me."

The director's wife said, "Didn't a spot open up today?"

I said, "No it didn't."

The director told me he'd check into it and get back to me. Two days later he told me I'd been accepted! And I remember laughing, because I knew it was God. I still didn't want to go, but I was excited because I knew I was finally doing God's will. And if it was God's will, then how could it be wrong?

I spent nine months without music or TV, I spent nine months studying the Bible, and I spent nine months finding out that Jesus really *is* the Great I Am! The God who made the universe, the One who said, "Let there be light," and there was light, humbled himself and came into the world as a man. Our Maker, who is so big and so powerful and so sovereign, loved us so much that he allowed himself to be tortured and hung on a cross in order to save us from our sin, and from hell. He did all this for *us!* Not because he had to— but because he *wanted* to, because he *loves* us! The moment this really sunk in, I started crying.

***"In the beginning was the Word,
and the Word was with God, and the
Word was God. All things were made by him,
and without him was not any thing made...
And the Word was made flesh
and dwelt among us..."***

(John 1:1, 3, 14 KJV)

When my time at Joshua was coming to an end, I began praying about what to do next. From the first month at the program, people had told me that God was going to use me to counsel drug addicts. I loved this idea, and I prayed that God would make it so. —But then I learned about an internship at a church— in *Hawaii! Yes! Thank You Lord!*

But God had something different in mind.

Ken Graves came to speak at Joshua. He told me I should come to the School of Leadership at his church— in *Maine!* He told me, "It's going to be really hard. You're not going to get a lot of sleep. You're not going to get a lot of time off. You're either going to be working, going to school, studying, preaching, or sleeping. "

So I said, "You got any other ideas?" I was NOT going to MAINE!

Then that thing started *bugging* me again.

Here in Maine, one of the things I'm doing is counseling drug addicts at the church's residential discipleship program. I get to hang out and love on the guys who are recovering from addictions, and I get to relate to them what I've learned. Some of them don't want to be here, but the guys who genuinely devote themselves to the Lord... well, seeing them grow is just so cool!

I now understand that that thing bugging me, is God's Spirit. I know how much he loves me, and I know he wants to give me the desires of my heart. (Psalm 37:4) When I was at Joshua I started praying about getting back into wrestling. I love wrestling, and it's always been my dream to be a wrestling coach.

Just last week, Ken said, "You know they might need help with the wrestling team..."

God is good.
He really is.
If you've got the Holy Spirit bugging you.
Just do it.
Don't argue.
There's no point.
He's always right.
Trust Him.
God is good.
He really is.

The best thing I've been able to accomplish with my own hands is almost killing myself. The best decisions I ever made got me into the worst places. How God can use someone like me, I still don't know. But he can. He is fully capable of running people's lives.

"For I know the plans
I have for you," declares the LORD,
"plans to prosper you and not to harm you,
plans to give you hope and a future. Then you
will call upon me and come and pray to me,
and I will listen to you. You will seek me
and find me when you seek me
with all your heart."
(Jeremiah 29:11-13 NIV)

Give Him your life. You won't be sorry.

To learn more about Hume Lake or Joshua,
log onto www.Humelake.org.
To learn more about the CC Central Maine
School of Leadership:
call (207) 991-9555

From Dealer to Healer

Chuck's Story

I got saved when I was sixteen,
but knowing the Lord and walking with him,
are two very different things.

It started with cigarettes when I was nine years old, and marijuana soon after that. Before I joined the Marine Corps, drugs were taking control of my life, and after I joined, I became thoroughly enslaved. I fell in with a bunch of hard core users and started shooting up, and the quantity we did was unbelievable. We heard of men dying from smaller amounts than what we were doing.

It wasn't long before I went AWOL (absent without leave) and I didn't plan on going back. —But then I recommitted my life to the Lord and turned myself in. That's when I found out, even if you crawl back and apologize, they still throw you in the brig.

Back with my buddies I started using again, and soon went AWOL again. This time, I somehow ended up at a Bible study in Costa Mesa, California. After the service, I went forward to talk to Pastor Chuck Smith about the Marines, and about the drugs, hoping that he would say, "*Oh yeah, you need to stay away from there you know*." But instead, he brought me over to his assistant pastor, who just *happened* to be a retired Marine Drill Instructor, who just *happen* to be some of the meanest guys in the Marine Corps! I braced myself for a severe chastening, but instead he was very nice, and he laid out scriptural reasons for why I needed to go back and serve my country.

So I went back, again, and got thrown in the brig,

again. This pattern repeated itself several times; Go AWOL, recommit to Jesus, turn myself in, get thrown in the brig, start using again. Out of my two years in the military, I spent ten months AWOL, ten months in prison, and six months good time.

Eventually, the Marines got fed up with me, and set me free.

But I was still in bondage. Back home in Oregon, I hooked up with a couple of friends and spent the next five years as a weekend junkie. We'd work all week, then get high all weekend. But the money we made working wasn't enough, so we started stealing anything that wasn't tied down. Canoes disappeared from the roofs of cars, lawnmowers vanished from front yards, trucks found themselves without radiators, and the telephone company was losing copper wire left and right. We made over a thousand dollars a week selling stolen goods, and it's a miracle we were never caught.

Then one day my sister asked if I wanted to move with her to Southern California. She and her husband had been praying for a long time, and they thought if they could get me away from my friends, maybe I'd stop using. And they were right.

I partied all the way down on the train, but the minute my feet hit the pavement, I felt the Lord telling me, *The party's over.* And from that moment, my drug use came to a screeching halt, my gutter street language disappeared, and my life changed completely. I was thrown in with a bunch of Christians and for *ten years* my life was Christ centered. I was completely free from the bondage of drugs and alcohol.

Until one night, when my uncle handed me a joint.

"Stand fast therefore in the liberty with which Christ has made us free, and do not again be held with the yoke of bondage."
(Galatians 5:1 MKJV)

As time went on, Chuck married a woman he met at church. But the marriage ended after three and a half years when his wife found out he was stealing from their house fund to buy pot. Soon after this, he married another woman he'd met at church. He told his second wife about the marijuana, but she had no idea the extent of it; he was smoking at least three or four joints every day. They had two boys and were together for several years before Chuck went back to work, and the problems escalated.

For three years my wife worked and I was Mr. Mom. I took good care of my boys, but I was still sneaking joints every chance I got. There was never a shortage of Visine or cologne at our house. For awhile, I got away with this, but then I went back to work.

I was working graveyard when I first snorted a small amount of crystal meth to help me stay awake. And I did stay awake, for *two days!* It wasn't long before I was snorting all the time. But I lied to myself. If I wasn't shooting, I wasn't using. This was a lie from the pit of hell.

My wife didn't have a clue what I was doing, but she knew something was up, because I went from a hefty one hundred-ninety pounds, to a skinny one-fifty in six months, and I started fighting with her all the time. Then one night I hauled off and hit her. So she got on the phone and had me hauled off to jail.

When I got out, I begged and pleaded and promised that I would never hit her again if she took me back. But I didn't keep my promise, and I found myself in jail, again. This time she didn't let me come home for two months, and when I did go back, I only managed to stay clean for two weeks.

Before she kicked me out, I lost my job. After she kicked me out, she handed me divorce papers. So I found myself with no family, no job, and no place to live. I managed to find a job, and a room in a little "share the bathroom down the hall" transient hotel. I wanted to clean myself up so I started going to a secular rehab program and gave up speed. But I tested positive for pot— and never went back. Then I found out the guy down the hall was a speed dealer.

So much for giving up speed.

For the next year, a third of my pay went for rent, a third went for my kids, and the other third went for my habit. But, after awhile, I felt if I didn't get away from there, I would die.

So I came up with a brilliant plan. I got all my stuff together and set out to go back-packing until I ran out of money. I brought my drug dealer along, and he brought an eight ball of speed, and we set out to climb Mt. Whitney, the tallest mountain in the United States. It's a six hour climb to the top, but it took us *four days!* We'd sleep till noon, do a couple of lines, walk for an hour or two, then set up camp and do more lines. When we finally got to the top, we were low on food and out of speed. We had two options: We could either ration our food and hike twenty miles a day for the next two days, or, we could turn around and go right back out. We hiked out in six and a half hours what took us four days to get in.

At this point, I decided to hitchhike up to Oregon to see if one of my brothers or sisters would take me in. But no one would have anything to do with me. I was nothing more than an emaciated human being, a stick rail of a person with sunken cheeks. No one was going to trust me, especially with their kids around. Every door was closed, and after a week, I hitchhiked back to Southern California. A guy I used to work with let me sleep on his couch for a couple of weeks, but then he found out I was back on drugs, and I found myself back on the street.

I called my wife and told her I was leaving the state. She wanted to know where I was going and I told her I was just going to hitchhike until I found something. It was New Year's weekend, 1996, and I hitchhiked down to Long Beach where I met up with my nephew and his wife. We partied all weekend, and then I called my wife again.

She'd been doing some research and she told me about a place called U-Turn for Christ. She said, "They'll take you. They're a drug and alcohol place and they're right over in Perris." I didn't want to listen to her. But she kept saying. "They *will* take you. I've already talked to them." And the more she talked, the more I realized— I had no other options.

My nephew dropped me off at the train station. I took the train, then the bus, and finally I had to walk a few miles overland. I smoked my last joint as I walked up to the place, and as I walked through the gate, I prayed, *"Lord if they accept me, I'm back for good."*

Sure enough, they took me in.

I thought I had to clean myself up before the Lord

would take me back, but I was wrong. In His infinite grace, He took a wretched, drug addicted, wife beating loser like me, and *He* did the cleaning. He took what the world had rejected, and turned me into a respectable human being whose life is now committed to serving Him, and serving others who find themselves in bondage to drugs and alcohol.

"Therefore if the Son shall make you free, you shall be free indeed."
(John 8:36 MKJV)

When I entered U-Turn, I'd known Jesus for thirty-five years, but knowing him and walking with him are two *very* different things. I always knew he existed. I could see him in nature and I accepted his presence. I acknowledged him like my shadow, but I was doing what *I* wanted to do. Walking with the Lord means to follow His ways, to do His will, and to obey His Word. And when you do this, you are free indeed. I started walking with the Lord on January 2, 1996, and I don't regret a single step.

"As you therefore have received Christ Jesus the Lord, so walk in him."
(Colossians 2:6 MKJV)

"Blessed are the undefiled in the way, who walk in the law of the LORD."
(Psalm 119:1 KJV)

Some time before going to U-Turn, my sister told my brother she'd given up and stopped praying for me. My little brother laid into her and said, “How *dare* you think my God can’t help him! He’s our brother and God can do *anything* and you need to be praying for him!” He convicted her, and she started praying. The day I walked into U-Turn was my sister's birthday. God heard those prayers and He brought me to U-Turn. Don’t ever give up on a family member, or anybody else. Just pray for them. Prayer *will* change things.

On average, the success rate for men who complete the U-Turn program is well above 50%, which is far more successful than secular rehab programs that don’t focus on God’s Word. **To learn more about U-Turn 4 Christ, visit their web site at www.uturn4christ.com**

In His infinite patience, the Lord freed Chuck. But amazingly, this wouldn’t be the last time God saved his neck.

In 2001, I came to Maine from California to open up another U-Turn. The first night I was at Calvary Chapel, the pastor introduced me to the congregation and explained what I was there to do. After the service, a man came up and welcomed me. He was a doctor, and he told me to let him know if there was anything he could do for me.

One night I saw him in church and asked if he’d take a look at the mole on my temple. He looked at it, but was more interested in looking at the lump on my neck, which was about an inch around and stuck out about an inch. He told me I should have it checked. But since I didn’t have any money, or insurance, I decided not to worry about it and I put it out of my mind.

But the doctor didn't forget. He was in a weekly Bible study with a group of surgeons and he told them about my situation. One of the surgeons told him to send me in and that he wouldn't charge me for the visit. So I went in and the doctor took a needle biopsy. I didn't understand what had happened, and when I left the hospital with a bandage on my neck, I thought the lump was gone.

But it wasn't gone, and a few days later I was called in to discuss the results of the biopsy. I was having a hard time understanding the doctor because he was using a lot of medical terms. He was saying the lump was malignant and that it had metastasized into my neck and that I was lucky it hadn't gone into my lymph nodes. I didn't have a clue what he was talking about and finally I interrupted him. "Should I be concerned about all of this?"

He chuckled and patted me on the shoulder and said, "Yeah. This is the Big One." He told me I had cancer, and that metastasized meant it had started somewhere else. He didn't like the look of my tonsils, so he was going to look at them the following week. I was a little choked up, but I thought I could tough it out, and I *wasn't* going to cry about it.

When I went back to the church, Sheila, the secretary, looked at me and said, "Well?" And when I said, "Its cancer," she started crying, and I started crying. And then Pastor Ken came in. When he found out what all the crying was about, he said, "You take my office and stay as long as you want and make all the phone calls you need."

So I got through the rest of that day, calling my family and friends, telling them I had cancer.

The following week, I went in for a tonsillectomy. They put me under and took out my right tonsil. And the doctor said, "We got it all." So, once again, I was under the impression that the problem had been taken care of. I thought the cancer was gone. But it turned out, he had gotten all the *original* cancer in the tonsil, but the metastasized cancer was still in my neck. —So they scheduled me for radiation.

Radiation is a weird thing. I was strapped down to a bed with a machine going over me— but *nothing* was happening. I could see nothing. I could feel nothing. But little by little, over time, my energy was completely drained and large ulcers were forming on the sides of my tongue. Eating became excruciatingly painful and my taste buds were dying. Ken and I would go out for lunch, but I couldn't eat. Nothing tasted good. I would take one bite, and Ken would get to eat the rest. I was devastated!

And because I couldn't eat, I had to drink Ensure, and that stuff was just *gagging* me! I forced myself to drink one or two cans a day, and lost thirty pounds in a month, then the doctor threatened to put me on IVs if I didn't maintain my weight. So I had to drink at least six cans of this disgusting stuff every day. And you know what, the radiation didn't kill all of my taste buds. The ones that could taste Ensure were still alive.

After about a month of radiation, the nurse asked if I was ready for pain medication. And because I used to be a heroin addict, a speed freak, a pot smoker- *and* a drunk, I kept putting it off. But then one day the doctor wrote a prescription for pain meds and I gave in. He put me on Oxycontin, which is a man made heroin. I had to take five mils every couple of hours- but as the weeks went by, the doctor said I could take two, then three.

The meds worked great for the pain, but there were side effects. My stomach was always upset, and I could barely keep my eyes open. I was afraid to sit in church, because I thought at any minute I would nod off and snore, or worse, fall out of my chair. In fact, I got to the point where I was so tired, I would fall asleep at red lights. The drug was messing up my mind and I didn't recognize the danger I was putting myself in. One day while driving, I had the guys from U-Turn behind me and it crossed my mind that if I started to go off the road, they would honk and wake me up!

Then one day I was giving the assistant pastor's daughter a ride home and I swear I did *not* nod off. But she told her dad I did, and when Pastor Ken heard about it, he said, “That's it, you’re moving in with me and Jeanette, and I’m going to be your driver from now on.” So I moved in with Ken.

Because of the nausea and the Ensure, I felt sick all the time. Ken has a Dodge pickup truck with a passenger handle on the windshield frame. We’d be driving along and without saying anything, I'd hang onto the handle, open the door, and heave out the side of the truck. Ken would be yelling, “Let me pull over! Let me pull over!” and to this day Ken says he never knew what those handles were for, until he had me in the truck.

And so it went for about another month; living at Ken’s, getting radiation, doing the Oxycontin, drinking the Ensure, and hanging from the truck handle.

When the radiation therapy ended after two months, I went in for a check-up. The doctor said I needed a *radical neck dissection!* They were going to cut away the whole right side of my neck from front to back! Radiation had failed. The lump was still there. You could see it. You could feel it. You could practically hang a hat on it!

I asked the doctor how long it would be before I

could travel to see my kids and he said, "See them before the operation, because if they see you after, it'll be too radical for them."

So he scheduled the operation. I had another MRI. And the next day, I boarded a plane for California.

The doctor said it would be at *least* six months before my taste buds came back, but amazingly, two weeks later, I was taking my kids out to restaurants, and eating a whole meal!

But I wouldn't eat ice cream. Before the radiation, I would eat about a half a gallon of ice cream every night, but after, it just wasn't the same. Someone asked me why and I said, "You know how ice cream dances on your tongue... well, it quit dancing." It was seven months before I started eating ice cream again.

After three weeks in California, I went back to Maine and found a message on my machine from the doctor's office. They wanted me to come in right away. So I called and the secretary said, "The doctor needs to talk to you. How soon can you get here?"

—Whatever God wanted to do was okay with me. I figured, if he wanted to take me home, he'd take me home, and if he wanted to use me with half a neck, he'd use me with half a neck. Actually, I was excited about the possibility of going home to be with the Lord. I never once prayed for healing. But the way the secretary told me to come right away had me worried. I thought maybe the MRI showed something worse, maybe the cancer had spread.

When I got to the office, I asked, "*What's up?* Is it good news or bad news?" The nurse smiled at me and said, "When the doctor came back from his vacation, he couldn't understand why he had you scheduled for surgery."

Just then, the doctor came in and started feeling

around on my neck. He asked if I could feel the lump and I said, "No, I thought I'd misplaced it!" In California I was trying to tell people about this lump, but I couldn't find it! Then the doctor told me that the last MRI showed *no trace* of the cancer. All it detected was some scar tissue from the radiation, but that was all! They were stumped by it.

The lump was still there when I'd finished radiation, but now it was completely gone! I said, "Well praise God! You wouldn't believe how many people have been praying for me!" It was true! *I* hadn't prayed for healing, but I had friends and family all over the world praying for me. I had friends in Maine, South Carolina, and Tennessee, family in California, Oregon, and Florida, and friends in India, Europe, and the Philippines all praying for me. And God answered their prayers. The cancer was gone! And this time, when the doctor said it was gone, I wasn't misunderstanding him. It was *gone!* There wasn't a trace to be found.

"...pray for one another, that you may be healed. The effectual fervent prayer of a righteous one avails much."
(James 5:16 MKJV)

And not only did the cancer disappear, the medical bills vanished right along with it. My doctor sent me a bill just so I could see it. It was thirty *thousand* dollars. St. Joe's hospital wrote off twenty or thirty thousand, and Eastern Maine Medical Center wrote off about the same!

My medical bills were close to a hundred thousand dollars, but I never had to pay a penny.

Five years after his ordeal
with cancer, Pastor Chuck is cancer free,
clean and sober, and still walking with the Lord.

And the ice cream just keeps on dancing.

Pastor Chuck says,

"Praise God!"

The Appointment

Kim's Story

I wanted to cancel the appointment. There was simply too much going on. There were only five shopping days left until Christmas, and I was *working* three of those days. Besides, the kids didn't really *need* their hair cut. Debbie wouldn't mind if I rescheduled, I knew she wouldn't. —I *really* wanted to cancel that appointment.

But I didn't.

I told Garrett and Jillian on the way to the salon that they were *not* going to stay to play with Samantha when we were done. We were going to go in, get their hair cuts done, and get out of there! Period.

When we arrived at Kid Kutters, the place was a madhouse. There were three other moms in the waiting area, and a total of nine kids, including mine, now playing loudly together all over the shop. To my relief, Debbie was able to take Jillian right away, and soon Garrett was in the chair having his turn. When he was done, I was ready to go.

But the kids begged. "Just five minutes, Mommy? *Please?* We never get to play with Samantha! And she's going to put in a movie. Please, Mommy? *Pleeeeease?"*

I looked over at Debbie's little seven year old, Samantha, a beautiful dark haired girl, and such a sweetheart. She was helping the kids get arranged around the little TV set and starting to hand out Christmas candies from a dish.

"Oh all *right*. But only *five minutes!"* —Little did I know they would be five of the most important minutes of my life. I walked over to the coat rack and got my kids' coats and boots ready so we could hurry right out— then I heard Debbie's voice. She was *panicked!*

"Oh my GOD! Somebody help me! She's CHOKING! Somebody help! Somebody HELP SAMANTHA!"

I looked over and saw Samantha clutching at her mother with a look of horror painted on her face. She was turning bright red. Now normally I'm kind of a nervous person, a real worrier, but as I looked over at them, a perfect peace came over me. It was a feeling of perfect protection and calm, as though someone else had taken control.

I parted the crowd and pointed at one of the moms. "Call 911. She isn't breathing!" I squatted down in front of Samantha. "I'm going to help you."

Debbie had collapsed in her chair and was turning green with panic.

I turned Samantha around, put my arms around her, and began to perform the Heimlich maneuver. I did it once, twice, three times. After the fourth, Samantha suddenly took a deep breath. I asked her, "Is it still in there?" She nodded yes. So I continued with the upward thrusts to her sternum. One— two— three. With this third one, a red and white peppermint candy shot out of her mouth and landed five feet away in the corner. She collapsed in my arms and I asked her, "Are you okay, honey?" She nodded yes, so I picked her up and put her in her mother's lap. —I think everyone in the shop was crying.

After my kids came over and hugged Samantha, and after everything was said and done, I had time to help my kids with coats and boots, get them out to the car, get them strapped into their car seats, and was ready to pull out— when the paramedics arrived. By that time, it would have been too late to save Samantha.

I really wanted to cancel that appointment— but I didn't. I felt compelled to keep it.

"I thank him who has given me strength, Christ Jesus our Lord, because he judged me faithful, appointing me to his service,"
(1 Timothy 1:12 ESV)

Words from a thankful Mom:

I pray all the time for the Lord to protect my children and I believe the Lord brought Kim here that day to save Samantha. She was the only one in the shop who knew the Heimlich maneuver. If she hadn't been here, Samantha wouldn't be here.

It was a miracle.

This incident changed me. I've always appreciated my daughter, she's a gift, but now my time with Samantha is even more precious. I take nothing for granted.

I love my job; I wouldn't be working with children if I didn't, but now, every time a child comes into my shop, I'm that much more aware of how very precious they are.

The day after Kim performed the Heimlich maneuver on Samantha, Debbie called the Red Cross to see about getting signed up for CPR classes. She told them what Kim had done, and they suggested she nominate Kim for the annual Hero's Award. Several months later, Debbie received a call. Kim had won!

I was so happy to get that call from the Red Cross! I'm just so ***HAPPY*** that she ***WON!*** *Because she saved my baby!*

Salt and Light

Elizabeth's Story

E-liz-a-beth (i liz' e beth), consecrated to God.
con-se-crate (kon' se krat'), *v.*, 1. to make or declare sacred; set apart or dedicate to the service of God.

(Elizabeth speaks in imperfect English with a Spanish accent.)

As a young girl in El Salvador, I live in a Christian home, but I never believe in God one hundred percent.

Until this happen.

I was, nineteen, married, pregnant— and I was thinking, God is not today, God is tomorrow.

I put myself before God.

We go to church a few times. But I don't really believe. Then one time the pastor ask us, will we have a Bible study in our home. So we say okay.

There was, many people in my house. Everybody is ready. We already pray, and everybody is waiting for me. I am busy cooking; making snacks, and a type of drink in a pressure cooker. It is made with corn meal and sugar inside a coffee can. The can heats inside a pot and it builds up pressure. A *lot* of pressure.

So the people wait, and I go into the bathroom to look at myself in the mirror. I am thinking, "Oh. I am so beautiful. I am *very* beautiful!"

I loved myself before God.

So I took my time.

I come back and I say, "Okay. I'm ready." —And I'm not thinking about what I'm doing— because I'm thinking about *me.*

"Pride goes before destruction, and a haughty spirit before a fall."
(Proverbs 16:18 MKJV)

I open the pressure cooker and the drink explode in my face.

In my country the hospital is far away. They want to take me but I say no, because I'm pregnant; they will put me on antibiotics, and it will harm the baby I think. So I refuse that.

That night, I don't sleep. My face is burning, burning, *burning* HOT.

The next day, a relative of my husband come and they take me to a witch. *A witch!* I try to block this out; it was *so ridiculous!* She speak in a strange language. And she give to us some cream, *Voo Doo* cream.

My face become— very infected.

Someone else give to me some cream from the pharmacy. My face get worse. Full of puss. Dripping. And I was very sick. Very sick and very depressed. So depressed— I don't care anymore.

I feel dead.

On the third day, I look like a monster. A black monster. Charcoal on my face. Very scary. Very scary and very dangerous.

I look in the mirror and I say, "I guess I'm not beautiful anymore."

My husband look at me and he say, "You know you will need plastic surgery."

The fourth day, the pastor come to my house. "You need to go to the hospital."

"No. I'm not going to the hospital."

"Do you mind if I pray for you?"

"Yeah. You can pray for me."

So he pray. He say, "I pray, God, You will give me some miracle that I can bring for this girl's face." He say I need to have faith. And I did. I was feeling confident.

Then he went home, and the next day he come back and he say, "You know I pray, and God lead me to look in a book. It opened just to the right page! It say to wash your face with salt and water and your skin will heal."

Salt water! You know how painful is that?

But I say, "Well... If you pray about it, God have a purpose for it. Let's do that."

Before he wash my face, we pray again. He pray for healing, but in my heart, I pray for forgiveness. I say, "I know God, that this is your day. I know you have called me to serve you. I give everything to you. Forgive me. I'm yours."

And I feel *light!* So light! And so happy! I never feel so happy in all my life! And the happiness last, for—*years!*

"Give joy to the soul of Your servant...For You, Lord, are good and ready to forgive, and rich in mercy to all those who call on You."

(Psalm 86:4-5 MKJV)

Then he put the cloth on my face. It was... so *refreshing!* Cooling. Like when you are very thirsty and you drink a BIG glass of water. Aaaaahhhhh! *So* relaxing! *Wonderful!* I want more, and more...

Every day for three days, he come to my house and he wash my face with salt water. On the third day, my face start to be dry, so we leave it alone.

Four days after this, my face is completely dry.

A month went by and my face was ugly. I had to walk with a veil over my face because people couldn't help looking at me. But now, I don't care, I don't feel shame. I feel content, and I don't care what I look like. I have God—and he fill me with joy!

I don't put myself before God anymore.

After awhile, I have my baby, and my face is normal again. Yes!

God is so good.

God is SO *good!*

He bring to me the pastor so I can have salt water to save my face, but *far* better, he bring to me Jesus, so I can have the *living water,* to save *me*.

"Jesus answered,
...the water that I shall give him shall
be in him a well of water springing
up into everlasting life."
(John 4:13-14 MKJV)

"...everyone who shall call
upon the name of the Lord
shall be saved."
(Acts 2:21 MKJV)

Words from Elizabeth

Always love God more than people.
Because no matter how much they love you,
they will always let you down.
God will never let you down.

It's very simple.
You just need to open your eyes and say,
“Oh. That's right. You're God!”
You've been there all my life!

He's so wonderful.

Knowing God.
It's like having huge piles of gold
that keeps piling and piling...
and you just want to give it away!
'Cause there's no place to put it!

Heaven

Lily's Story

Five year old Lily was afraid to go to heaven, because she didn't know what it would be like. At the age of three, she had been diagnosed with cancer throughout her body. Lily underwent two surgeries to remove a large tumor from her abdomen, and faced two years of chemotherapy— but the cancer was still spreading. The hospital staff told the family, all they could do now, was make her comfortable.

"He's fishing! He's fishing in heaven!" Lily told her nurse one day when she entered the room.

"What are you talking about, Lily?" the nurse asked.

"The boy next door! He's happy now! He's fishing in heaven!"

There was no way Lily could have known the boy in the next room had died. There was a picture in his room of him propped up holding a fishing pole— but Lily had never been in his room.

Perhaps this was God's way of easing Lily's fears about heaven.

The little girl continued to get worse. And one day, when her mother was with her, Lily started counting. Gazing up into the corner, she counted, "One, two, three..." She got as far as ten, then started over— because that was as high as she could count.

She did this several times.

Finally her mother asked, "What are you doing Lily?"

She answered, "I'm counting the angels, Mommy."

The very next day, Lily found out for herself, what heaven is like.

"And God shall wipe away all tears from their eyes; and there shall be no more death, neither sorrow, nor crying, neither shall there be any more pain: for the former things are passed away."
(Revelation 21:4 KJV)

The nurse who shared this story, said she's heard of at least three other children under the age of six who saw angels a day or two before they died.

The Gift

Joan's Story

I strolled through the aisles of the small town grocery store, gathered several items into my cart, then headed for the checkout. The cashier totaled up and bagged my order and I paid her.

But before I could step away, she piped up. "Are you sure you aren't forgetting anything?"

Thinking this was weird, I gave her a look. "Ah... I don't think so."

She flashed a brilliant smile then reached beneath the small counter and pulled up a large fully decorated Christmas tree. "Here. You forgot this. It's free!"

I stood with my mouth open. "Are you sure?"

"Yes. Take it. It's yours."

"Thank you!" I said as I carefully balanced the tree in my cart and began pushing it away from the counter.

"Are you sure you aren't forgetting anything?" It was the cashier again.

This time I smiled in anticipation and repeated, "I don't think so."

Again she reached beneath the counter and this time brought up the biggest, most beautiful Easter basket I had ever seen. Intricately decorated with sparkling ribbons, it nearly overflowed with chocolates and candies. My eyes were wide and her eyes sparkled as she handed it over. I could hardly believe my good fortune.

Quickly I began to push the cart homeward. Somehow I knew I needed to get home before I could dig into my treasures. I rushed along and thought to myself, *I need to get home, get home, get home...*

But before I could get there, I woke up— and once again, I was a tiny girl snuggled beneath the covers of my bed. Excitement melted into disappointment as I reached down and plucked Teddy from the floor. I hugged him tight and squeezed my eyes shut— but sleep would not come. My treasures were gone. Oh *why* hadn't I eaten the candies? *Why* did I have to get home first?

I was not quite four years old when I had this dream, yet I remember it still today, some thirty-five years later. I was an adult in the dream, and it was so real. How could I, a tiny child, know what it felt like to be an adult? I always thought this was the reason why I never forgot the dream— but perhaps there was a greater purpose.

Many years passed, and I don't remember exactly when I first began listening to the Christian radio network, CSN International, but once I started, I was *hooked.* I'd always wanted to read the Bible, but I'd never made it past Genesis on my own. CSN was a gold mine! What a blessing! I learned so much from the pastors on the radio: the meaning of repentance, evidence for creation, the inerrancy of scripture, why there is evil in the world... and that Calvary Chapel pastors are all just a little bit nutty. But this is okay, because God uses the foolish things of the world to confound the wise. Right? (I learned that from CSN too.) —But seriously, I was hearing the word, my faith was growing, and I recommitted my life to Jesus.

Then one night as I sat listening to a teaching about the fact that salvation cannot be earned, it hit me! That dream I'd had all those years ago contained a message! It was about the gift. *The* gift. Jesus.

I *paid* the cashier for the groceries, but the tree and the basket were *free*. I hadn't done anything to earn them. All I needed to do was accept them. A Christmas tree and an Easter basket, symbols of Jesus' arrival on earth, and of his resurrection from the dead!

To be saved, all we need to do is accept the *free gift*, which God holds out with a smile.

"For by grace are ye saved through faith; and that not of yourselves: it is the gift of God: Not of works, lest any man should boast."
(Ephesians 2:8-9 KJV)

As a tiny child, God planted the message of the Gospel in my heart. Subsequently, it wasn't until I became an adult (as I was in the dream) that I accepted Jesus as my Savior and the hole in my heart was filled to overflowing with His Spirit (like the candies in the basket).

And there's one more thing I believe the dream revealed: Those of us who have accepted Jesus, will not truly taste the gifts God has given us, until we leave this world, and join him in eternity.

Wouldn't it be just like our precious Savior, to have that beautiful Easter basket waiting for me, when I *finally* do make it home?

My Shield

Daniel's Story

"The LORD is
my strength and my shield;
my heart trusted in him,
and I am helped..."
(Psalm 28:7 KJV)

I was riding on the top of the vehicle when the bomb went off. A road side IED. I thought for sure I was going to die.

But I didn't.

It was as though there was an invisible shield all around me. The debris was flying at my face, and I was knocked unconscious, but nothing hit me— nothing but a tiny piece of shrapnel that just clipped the end of my nose.

Some of the other guys were killed.

I know without a doubt, that God protected me.

"Keep me, O LORD,
from the hands of the wicked;
preserve me from the violent man..."
(Psalm 140:4 KJV)

Daniel was twenty-three years old and serving as a United States Army medic on his third tour in Iraq, when the roadside bomb exploded underneath his vehicle.

After this all of my buddies kept asking me, "Why are you always so calm? Why aren't you afraid?" I told them, "Because I truly trust in the Lord."

"God says, 'I will save those who love me and will protect those who acknowledge me as LORD.'"
(Psalm 91:14 GNB)

Tracy's Song

Joanie's Story

Matthew didn't know how Tracy had died;
that's what made the song so amazing.

A phone call came into the Hampden Police Department early that Wednesday morning in November of 2002. An abandoned car had been found on a tiny dirt road behind Green Lake. The police had been looking for the car, and its owner, since the Friday before.

Was there any hope that the young mother would be found alive?

Tracy was my cousin, but I considered her more of a sister. She was dark and pretty, with long beautiful eyelashes and a gentle way about her. When we were very little, everyone called us "*kissing* cousins," because that's how we greeted one another. As we grew, we shared time and secrets, laughter and heart aches, and we stayed up late every chance we got, talking and giggling— until, inevitably, she would fall asleep on me while I was still talking.

Tracy was my favorite cousin, and my best friend.

But when we reached our teen years her life was thrown into turmoil and our friendship began to suffer. Both of her parents passed away and she began to cling more and more to her boyfriend. We kept in touch, but there was a wall between us, and she no longer opened up to me.

As an adult, Tracy appeared to have her life together. She was smart and creative and loved the out of doors almost as much as she adored her two boys. As a successful accountant for the hospital, she always bought the best and didn't seem to have a want in the world. But all that glitters is not gold.

Tracy had endured the most painful year of her life before disappearing. Crushed under the weight of a failed marriage, she desperately reached out to anyone and everyone. She hadn't had a decent night's sleep in months and was almost always on the verge of tears. In an effort to stay healthy for her sons, she forced herself to eat, but grew thinner by the day. Counseling, and antidepressants, did little to lift the weight of hopelessness— and I will never forget the words she whispered to me over the phone one night.

"I want my mother."

—But her parents had been gone for years.

Everywhere she turned, there seemed to be contradicting advice. Some told her to believe in herself. Others told her to trust in God. She attended church with me a few times, but mostly just stared blankly, or cried. She told me she had been listening to K-Love (a Christian radio station) in her car and that she had tried to "give it over to Jesus," but that it hadn't helped. She didn't *feel* any better for doing so.

But I began to notice changes in her. She said she'd been praying that God would help her to be strong and she had felt renewed strength at those moments when she most needed it. She also mentioned she couldn't believe how much corruption there was on TV. This was something she had never noticed before.

It seemed her heart was being changed. She was doing better emotionally, smiling more and crying less, and I began to believe that she would pull through and be okay. I began to see glimpses of the Tracy I knew as a child— my favorite cousin and my best friend.

But then shortly after experiencing a crisis, she became unresponsive, and simply disappeared, leaving a host of family and friends frantically searching.

The search team quickly assembled at the site of the abandoned car. Hours later, a hound picked up her scent and found her. She was up on a little hill deep in the forest. Apparently she had become tired and sat down to rest under a tree.

An empty bottle of sleeping pills was found in the car.

Friends and family came from all over the country to attend Tracy's funeral. The pastor spoke comforting words to a crowded room and gave a presentation of the Bible as a guide for life. Smiling images of a beautiful Tracy rolled by on the TV screen. People shared songs and stories— and tried to understand.

A few days later my husband was compiling a CD of songs from the funeral to send to Tracy's siblings, and for the first time, we realized, one of the songs not only mirrored Tracy's state of mind in the months before she died, but it also described Tracy's death. It had been sung by the pastor's son, Matthew, and it contained words which could have come directly from Tracy in her last moments of life. I was curious to find out how Matthew had found a song which so perfectly described the situation, but when we asked him, he was amazed to see how the song mirrored her death. He hadn't known how Tracy had died. —He'd felt strongly that God wanted him to sing that particular song, but he'd had no idea why.

The song is by The David Crowder Band and is entitled, *All That I Can Say.*

Tracy was walking through the woods, alone, after taking a bottle of sleeping pills. The drugs began to take effect. The song begins, "*Lord I'm tired, so tired from walking, and Lord I'm so alone. And Lord the dark is creeping in, is creeping up to swallow me. I think I'll stop, and rest here awhile. --This is all that I can say right now. This is all that I can give. That's my everything.*

She must have been calling out to God as she sat under the tree and began to fade from consciousness. The song goes on to say, "*Oh and did you see me crying? And did you hear me call your name? Wasn't it you I gave my heart to? I wish you'd remember where you set it down.*"

The Bible tells us that God will never leave us or forsake us. As she released her final breath, Tracy became aware that she was *not* alone. The song's last stanza says, "*I didn't notice you were standing here. I didn't know that that was you holding me. I didn't notice you were crying too. I didn't know that that was you washing my feet.*"

It was raining on that cold November day, and as Tracy sat huddled under the tree, her eyes were opened and she suddenly became aware, that the drops of water falling upon her feet, were the very tears of God.

"… because God has said,
'Never will I leave you; never
will I forsake you.'"
(Hebrews 13:5 NIV)

"The Lord is close to the
brokenhearted and saves those who
are crushed in spirit."
(Psalm 34:18 NIV)

The following scripture
is taken from the Gospel of John,
but it is also true for,
This Miracle.

***"... Jesus performed
many other miracles which are not
written down in this book.***

***But these have been
written in order that you may believe
that Jesus is the Messiah, the Son of God,
and that through your faith in him
you may have life."***
(John 20:30-31 GNB)

It’s simple. Have faith in Jesus, who died on the cross for your sins, that you might have life. —Everlasting life. It's a free gift! All you need to do is reach out and accept it. If you have never had your sins forgiven, and do not know that you will go to heaven when you die, you can pray a prayer something like the following:

Dear Father in heaven,

I need forgiveness. I believe that Jesus came and died on the cross so my sins might be forgiven. Please forgive me. And Lord Jesus, please come into my heart and change me. Help me live for you.

Amen.

If you do not know the Lord well enough to trust him with your eternal spirit, get to know him.

Read the Bible.

Want to hear about more miracles?
Read the Bible.

If you have a miracle
you would like to have considered
for *This Miracle-2*
contact Joan Hileman at
joaniehileman@gmail.com

To order more copies of *This Miracle:*
send your order to:
105 Fruit Street
Bangor, ME 04401

Include your name, address, phone, email.
Make checks payable to Joan Hileman

Books are $10.00 plus S&H

Shipping and Handling costs:
1-2 books- $3.00
3-4 books- $4.00
5-6 books- $5.00

Books are also available in the
Calvary Chapel Bookstore,
at 154 River Road, Orrington, ME

Printed in the United States
204182BV00002B/367/P

9 780977 147458